What law enforcement professionals are saying about *Emotional Survival for Law Enforcement* . . .

"If our profession has been shaped by a handful of pioneers, whose insights have provided a path forward to improve the quality of life for our people and the many communities they serve, Dr. Kevin Gilmartin is one of those few pioneers. Kevin has spent the last forty years sharing the development of a mentally and emotionally resilient compass for our people, as we attempt to move our organizations in the right direction while serving our communities. Kevin understands, as do some leaders in many professions, that equipment, task-based training, and resources are important, but what is vital is the development of the person. Gear can only get you so far in our business. I have been blessed to work closely with Kevin and have learned from his passion, tutelage, and insights. Take the time to enjoy this recent addition to Kevin's work, and then please share Kevin's work with your people."

Steven Pitts
Chief of Police (Ret)
Reno (NV) Police Department

"The first time I heard Dr. Kevin Gilmartin compare the overweight police officer to the bear, getting ready to hibernate in the fall, I said, "Wow, That's it!" Of all of Dr. Gilmartin's great stories. I believe that the one about bear is the most important to law enforcement today. So nice to see the hungry, insulin-resistant bear featured in the new version of *Emotional Survival for Law Enforcement*. Keep your cortisol and insulin levels low, Ladies and gentlemen. Don't become Kevin's bear!"

E. James Greenwald, MD

"The unique and increased value of this book . . . is that it can easily be revisited periodically. There are many occasions where reading (and re-reading) this book can be immensely beneficial—these include when an officer is hired, reassigned, and/or promoted. From a command perspective, this book provides insights which can directly influence how certain management decisions are made and, sometimes more importantly, delivered. Finally, this book provides guidance to agency heads and senior management as to the tone that must be set in order to increase survivors and decrease victims within their organizations."

Ann Marie Doherty
Superintendent (Ret.)
Boston Police

"I have been through Dr. Gilmartin's *Emotional Survival* training at least twice in my career and I found his lessons on surviving a law enforcement career the most valuable tool to my success and emotional survival both professionally and personally. . . . This book should be required reading for all new police officers and their loved ones."

Douglas L. Bartosh
Chief of Police and Director of Public Safety (Ret.)
Scottsdale, Arizona

"As a twenty-six-year veteran of law enforcement, I have had the opportunity to read many books and observe many trainers. *Emotional Survival* is a work of art! This book is perhaps the best law enforcement–related reading I have ever experienced. Whether you have twenty minutes on the job or twenty years, this book will make you a better officer and a better person, and just might save your life. Any person who wears a badge must read this book to better understand the climate of the profession. Dr. Kevin Gilmartin's experience and background in this field make him a definite asset to the law enforcement community and their families. Kevin has hit a home run with *Emotional Survival* and will ultimately impact thousands of lives."

Sergeant Alan Green
Los Angeles Police Department (Ret.)
Past President, National DARE Officers Association

"If you are a law enforcement officer concerned you are losing the spirit and passion that attracted you to this career, or a leader concerned about the attitude and well-being of your troops, then you will profit from the common-sense lessons of this book.

Dr. Kevin Gilmartin is nationally recognized not only for his groundbreaking work on the emotional survival of law enforcement officers, but also for his unique ability to captivate and personalize his message to a room full of cops. From his classroom comes this book, which captures the essence of the concepts and includes true stories which bring life to Gilmartin's material.

To this day, I remember glancing toward some of my grizzled sergeants as Gilmartin spoke. From the expressions on their faces, I knew Gilmartin's words were reaching them on a personal level.

Later, several of these supervisors openly acknowledged that Gilmartin was describing them and their life. The timing could not have been better, as our department was six months into a complete organizational change. To say officers and their supervisors were not happy with the reorganization is an understatement. Indeed, many supervisors saw themselves as victims, reeling from a new role, wearing newly designed uniforms and responsible for meeting new expectations.

A twenty-year cop himself, Gilmartin speaks a language cops can relate to. Supervisors were unanimous in their recommendation to bring Gilmartin back to address all our officers, which we did with as much success. My concern on Dr. Gilmartin's departure was sustaining what we had achieved. Months from now, I wondered, would we fall back into the same old behavior patterns and again see ourselves as victims? While the old behavior patterns did not return to previous levels, it was clear we needed a resource to periodically revisit the concepts of emotional survival.

Dr. Gilmartin's book, *Emotional Survival for Law Enforcement*, is the tool we need to keep focused on the emotional well-being of our personnel. In addition, it provides those uninitiated to Gilmartin's concepts the opportunity to experience his dynamic class as he guides us step-by-step through the personal challenges faced by every cop.

Armed with Gilmartin's book, officers can learn to successfully cope with one of the toughest jobs in a free society. Law enforcement can be a rewarding career that leaves one fulfilled, not bitter, caring, not isolated, and most important, a survivor, not a victim. Gilmartin's work is a significant tool to help us achieve this goal.

Mention 'survival class' to a young officer and he will invariably assume you are speaking of 'street survival.' Gilmartin makes a compelling case that an officer's emotional survival is every bit as important. If we fail to recognize this fact, it is very possible that the end result may be the loss of an officer, not to the streets, but to his own lack of emotional coping skills. The combination of officers educated in emotional survival coupled with strong leadership dedicated to making these issues a priority will produce stronger organizations and healthier officers. This is the essence of Dr. Gilmartin's landmark book."

Paul N. Conner
Chief of Police
Round Rock Police Department, Texas
Deputy Chief (Ret.)
Las Vegas Metropolitan Police Department

"I wish that someone would have talked about *Emotional Survival* with me during my career! Dr. Kevin Gilmartin's book would have helped me survive the politics of being a career cop. I certainly would have been better prepared to understand and help others as I rose through the ranks. Dr. Gilmartin's book should be part of the academy training as well as part of each and every promotional process. In fact, the politicians should read this."

Assistant Chief David S. Butzer (Ret.)
Portland Police Bureau
Portland, Oregon

"Having listened to Kevin Gilmartin over the years, I fully embrace what he states. Because the other day, I watched a young officer die. His death came about slowly over several months, but I am sure that it started a long time ago. He did not die a physical death but a professional one.

Standing in the holding area of the Clark County Detention Center, I watched as the police vehicles came and went. Then I looked up and saw one of my own officers under my command being led into the jail in handcuffs. He looked at me and I looked at him. I was looking for the young cop that he once was. He looked very scared. As we led him into the jail in which he started his career in law enforcement and put him through the booking process, I wondered what compromises he made. During that month, my officer was one of several in our agency that had been arrested for felony crimes. The arrest of the officers was of course the top story in the local media. They should be held accountable for their actions by our justice system.

Reality is that if we had several officers killed by gunfire in the line of duty in one month, the entire agency would be mobilized. I am sure that new training on tactics and officer survival would be rolled out. We would make sure that every recruit learned the lessons of the tragedy. In short, nothing would stop us from teaching the lessons to save the officers' lives on the streets.

But these officers died a professional death this month. We in law enforcement should be mobilizing. Every aspect of the officers' careers should be examined, and the lessons learned should be taught to avoid future casualties. The lessons learned and taught about *Emotional Survival* need to be taught in every class of new recruits and to every officer working. The need to do so is great. We as a profession need to consider emotional survival as a part of officer survival."

Gary Schofield
Captain (Ret.)
Las Vegas Metropolitan Police Department
U.S. Marshal District of Nevada

"*Emotional Survival* is an incredible book about the journey through the maze of police work. If you're a frontline officer, supervisor, or command officer, you will see yourself in this book. It is the first book I have read that describes what really happens to police officers in their careers, with incredible insight into the stress and difficulties of being a police officer. Dr. Kevin Gilmartin sets out proactive strategies for police officers and their families to survive the most dangerous profession."

Brian Adkin
President, Ontario Provincial Police Association
Ontario, Canada

"The material in this book changes lives. It does so by affixing responsibility for one's life exactly where it should be, on the individual, removing 'victim' status. We have seen miraculous, immediate changes in individuals who finally see who the real thief of their lives is—themselves. By following Kevin's advice, people become whole again. We, personally, and the law enforcement community, in general, owe Kevin a tremendous debt of gratitude for keeping us on track."

Barb Harris
Illinois State Police (Ret.)
and
Chief John W. Harris
Springfield Police Department, Illinois (Ret.)
Assistant Chief Tucson Police Dept (Ret.)
Chief of Police Springfield Police Dept, Illinois (Ret.)
Chief of Police Yankton, SD

"*Emotional Survival* should be required reading for all candidates and their families."

Edward Davis
Commissioner (Ret.)
Boston Police Department, Massachusetts

EMOTIONAL SURVIVAL FOR LAW ENFORCEMENT

REVISED EDITION

EMOTIONAL SURVIVAL FOR LAW ENFORCEMENT

A Guide for Officers and Their Families

REVISED EDITION

Kevin M. Gilmartin, Ph.D.

E-S Press

This book is dedicated to the law enforcement professionals who serve and protect each of us daily. I only hope that in some small way, it helps officers and their families complete the difficult journey through a law enforcement career with their relationships, families, and positive professional attitudes intact, and that it helps keep good people good.

Contents

Acknowledgments xv

Preface to the Revised Edition xvii

Foreword xix

1   The Journey through Law Enforcement 1

2   Officer Survival 7

3   Are the Changes Inevitable? 17

4   What Is Actually Taking Place? 23

5   Hypervigilance 41

6   The Hypervigilance Biological Rollercoaster 57

7   Long-Term Effects of Hypervigilance 87

8   How to Become an Emotional Survivor 133

About the Author 189

Acknowledgments

I would like to express my appreciation to the following mentors, colleagues, and family members without whose guidance and support this book would not be possible: Col. Harold E. Russell, PhD, who was willing to share his accumulated wisdom earned over more than half a century as both a military and police psychologist and who helped direct the formative years of my professional career; Alexis Artwohl, PhD, and Chief David Butzer for their collegial review and suggestions; Melanie Mallon for her editorial expertise; Randy Schultz of DesignPro Graphics for his creative design of this book; Jennifer M. Gilmartin-Garnand, MD, and Colleen F. Gilmartin, JD, for the dedication and commitment they show to their respective professions and the value they add to their parents' lives; and Anne M. Baustian-Gilmartin, WBW, for her continuing love, support, and assistance over the last four decades.

Preface to the Revised Edition

It's approaching two decades since the release of the initial publication of *Emotional Survival for Law Enforcement: A Guide for Officers and Their Families.* Over the span of those years, I have been honored and somewhat taken aback by the number of law enforcement professionals and their partners who have contacted us and related that the book made them aware of how they were conducting their lives both personally and professionally. They found the information to help them in finding a work-life balance.

As an author, receiving this correspondence is very gratifying. It also led to returning to the basic question that motivated the initial writing of the book:

> *What information would you like law enforcement professionals and their families to receive to make the journey through the career easier?*

In the initial version of the book, my goal was to explain the many aspects of the Hypervigilance Biological Rollercoaster® and spell out some possible resolution strategies. That remains a primary goal in this revised edition; however, over the years since the release of the book, I have become aware of a field of information about the cost of a policing career that appears to be receiving virtually no attention in the training of law enforcement.

I first became aware of this field of information about fifteen years ago when conducting a class for law enforcement and firefighters attending a conference in Reno, Nevada. One of the other conference presenters was speaking on premature death syndromes in public safety professionals. The presenter, Dr. James Greenwald, captured my attention while summarizing cases and asking questions such as "Why did this apparently healthy thirty-year old officer die of a heart attack?" "Why did these officers gain, on the average, twenty-five pounds since graduating from the Police Academy, even though, less than a decade ago, they were in excellent health? These officers were now on a path toward type 2 diabetes, as well as an increased risk of heart disease and stroke."

I approached Dr. Greenwald after his presentation, and we began discussing the interaction between police behavioral patterns and metabolic health. Soon the relationship expanded to a significant number of physicians, health scientists, and law enforcement leaders who were interested in giving police officers information on the physical effects encountered throughout their careers. Although the information was clearly available, it appeared siloed, virtually unheard of in the law enforcement world.

My goal in releasing this revised version of *Emotional Survival for Law Enforcement* is to link the impact of the very necessary hypervigilant state for officer safety with potentially life-changing disease processes.

My goal is to have the law enforcement professional prevent these disease processes and become not only an *emotional survivor* but also a *physical survivor*. The old adage that "you cannot solve a problem if you don't even know what the problem is" played a major role in my motivation.

I hope in some small way, this information lets law enforcement professionals make more self-directed decisions about how their life can function and implement strategies in the best interests for them and their loved ones.

—Kevin M. Gilmartin, PhD
Tucson, Arizona
February 2021

Foreword

If you're a cop, you're going to love this book. It could change your life. It might even *save* your life, your career, your home life.

If you're not a cop, you'll still love it because the ideas in this book could certainly apply to you too. Maybe you're in a relationship with a cop or have a highly demanding career that puts you on the "biological rollercoaster" ride, a concept that stems from Dr. Gilmartin's brilliant insight into the cost of public safety work and other high-stress occupations.

Author Kevin Gilmartin, PhD, is eminently qualified to write about emotional survival for law enforcement because he has lived it, studied it, researched it, and taught it. He is one of America's very few "cop docs." After earning his PhD in clinical psychology, he was a career deputy sheriff with the Pima County Sheriff's Office (PCSO), in Arizona. He began work at Pima County in 1974, retiring from the sheriff's department in 1995.

In 1982 he was nationally recognized for his work in hostage negotiations when he was selected as one of America's ten best "Police Officers of the Year" by *Parade Magazine*. Other operational activities during his deputy sheriff career included assisting investigators, criminal profiling, crisis interventions with emotionally disturbed persons, and dealing with extremist groups. The article he wrote on religious extremist groups, "The Lethal Triad," is still used in counter-terrorism training.

A true police psychologist is a rare breed in itself, and Dr. Gilmartin was one of the early pioneers in this highly specialized area. He was invited to write articles for leading publications and developed one of the nation's earliest police behavioral sciences units in the Tucson metro area. Although his initial interest was in operational work, his work in counseling police officers and their families soon led him to the realization that one of the most critical and ignored areas in law enforcement is the emotional toll this stressful occupation takes on its own people, and his focus turned increasingly to this area.

As a deputy sheriff and doctor living, working, and studying the unique world of cops and their families, he developed a penetrating insight into the daily work life of cops. He came to see how it insidiously dismantled the personal lives, health, happiness, and careers of officers who weren't prepared to cope with the unique demands of the law enforcement lifestyle. These officers and their family members became emotional casualties. Dr. Gilmartin was determined to do something that could help them become emotional survivors instead.

Fortunately for law enforcement at large, Dr. Gilmartin is a gifted trainer, who started training early in his career and soon became inundated with requests for training from across North America. After retiring from the PCSO, he was able to devote all his efforts to taking his message on the road internationally and is teaching as many officers as he can about the hazards of the wild biological rollercoaster ride, a ride that can end in disaster if officers don't learn to manage it.

I first heard Dr. Gilmartin speak at the International Association of Chiefs of Police (IACP) conference in 1993. I was instantly impressed by two things: This guy really *knows* what he's talking about, and he is *fun* to listen to. Not only is he highly entertaining, his message is clear, straightforward, and easy to understand. His life-changing advice is practical and simple to apply once you understand the concept of the Hypervigilance Biological Rollercoaster®.

When he isn't helping cops, Dr. Gilmartin chases steers and enjoys the cowboy lifestyle on his small horse ranch in Arizona. He and his wife, Anne, are avid team ropers.

As a law enforcement trainer myself, I, like Dr. Gilmartin, travel all over North America training cops. Because I admire his work, I usually mention Dr. Gilmartin's name and encourage officers to attend his training if they get the chance. Time after time officers have come up to me during the breaks to tell me they had been fortunate enough to listen to Dr. Gilmartin speak in person or on his videotape. They rave about how entertaining and informative the class was, but, more important, they tell me that hearing him speak changed their lives. Many of the older veterans wistfully tell me, "Better late than never, but I wish I had heard his talk at the beginning of my career."

Now Dr. Gilmartin has put his message in print in a book that is not only profound but almost as entertaining as he is in person. So enjoy, and go become an emotional survivor.

—Alexis Artwohl, PhD,
coauthor of *Deadly Force Encounters*

The Journey through Law Enforcement

For many men and women, the actual journey through a law enforcement career begins with the arrival of the letter announcing acceptance into the upcoming recruit academy class. With the exception of the actual day of academy graduation, this letter may bring on one of the happiest moments of a law enforcement officer's career. Receiving word of acceptance into the academy signifies both a major accomplishment and a starting point. After months, maybe years, of trying—studying, testing, taking oral boards—recruits finally have a chance to start their careers as officers, careers they may have wanted for some time and ones to which they will demonstrate significant commitment and dedication. They are entering careers that in many ways will define major parts of their lives for decades to come. Enthusiasm, idealism, and motivation are the emotions of the day.

These positive emotions remain throughout the demands of academy training, and they carry the recruits through a physically and mentally challenging few months. Endless hours of classroom instruction, academic tests, and training in physical fitness, defensive tactics, pursuit driving, EMS, and firearms all combine to fill the next few months of the law enforcement recruit's life. Although the academy experience is demanding, both physically and mentally, police officers in training see it in a positive light. This starting point is full of new experiences and new relationships. Recruits eagerly await graduation day and the chance to get out on the streets. Graduation day itself is a time of high spirits, during which recruits feel both a tangible sense of accomplishment for getting through the academy and the promise that an exciting and fulfilling career is just beginning.

The relationships among new recruits, formed during the trying times at the academy, can flourish over years of shared service as officers on the streets—often they develop into lifetime friendships. The intensity and extent of the relationships that occur among officers can be found in few other occupational fields. Despite the positive and supportive nature of the friendships that typify the early stages of a police career, however, not all changes taking place in the new officer's world are equally positive.

One of the first costs of the journey through the police career can be the old friendships, the ones that predate police work.

One of the first costs of the journey through a police career can be the old friendships, the ones that predate law enforcement. These friendships can be put on the back burner, and over time, these nonpolice friends may perceive their old friend, now an officer, as pulling back, not available, or only running around with their cop friends. Sometimes these friendships are the first loss brought on by police work, but this loss typically goes unnoticed by the new officer, who is caught up in an exciting new career.

Learning on the Job

Law enforcement is an entirely new world for the young officer. Not only is the career new, but the job itself is fun with a capital F. New officers focus on their mission to be the best officers they can be. They have so much to learn to become competent cops, most of which they learn from the older wiser cops, the ones who have been there and done that. The older veteran cops have paid their dues and are in a position to assist the young officer in obtaining full citizen membership in the police culture.

The reality is that although these more experienced officers really do know how to work the streets, often, tragically, that's the only part of their lives that does work effectively. When older officers are on the job, they know how to make decisions and handle situations. They appear competent and confident. Because the rookies' focus is almost exclusively on learning the job, they may see the shortcomings and failures in the veteran officers' personal lives as insignificant, if they notice them at all. From their predecessors, the next generation of officers learns how to handle the streets, but not necessarily how to handle their *personal lives* in their new profession. These veterans point the way and guide the journey from rookie to experienced fellow officer; however, the message passed along by veterans, many times, is an incomplete message for the overall transition. It focuses primarily on how to do the job—how to become a fellow cop who can be trusted and counted on under extremely demanding situations. The trust of other officers does not come easily for the rookie—earning it can be an uphill battle. For some new officers, the transition to the streets is significantly harder than the previous demands of the training academy. Being accepted and trusted by the other, experienced officers is, for most new officers, the major goal during the first year or two of their careers. This goal is earned only when the new officers can demonstrate that they can be counted on in tough situations, that they can be trusted when the chips are down.

Idealistic Rookie to Cynical Veteran

As the new officer's career continues, he or she can learn to rely, almost exclusively, on the support and friendship of other officers, a tendency that begins during the intense bonding at the academy. The officer doesn't make a conscious decision to abandon old friendships—it's just a matter of time before they seem to fade away. There are so many things to do and learn and so little time left for socializing with old friends. The demands of shift work scheduling only further impact the day-to-day life of the new officer. As the first year of the career draws to a close, officers may find themselves distant and alienated from social networks and friendships that existed prior to joining the force. Much of the experience earned by the law enforcement officer is done by surviving intense emotional and challenging situations. Bonding occurs between the cops that have shared those experiences.

As the years of a police career continue to pass, officers can experience social isolation from *everyone* except other cops. Positive outlooks and emotions are often replaced by dark, moody, negative views of the world. Although officers can experience their professional lives growing and expanding, on too many occasions their personal lives become fragmented and disrupted. Although work relationships can be supportive and available, personal relationships can become strained, distant, and dysfunctional. For almost all law enforcement officers, the career begins from a position of enthusiasm, motivation, and idealism, but the journey over the years from new recruit to experienced officer produces changes. Idealism can become cynicism, optimistic enthusiasm can become pessimism, and the easygoing young recruit can become the angry and negative veteran police officer.

The Job, the Whole Job, and Nothing but the Job

Anyone exposed to the police experience, either as an officer or someone who cares about an officer, can comment on how this journey through the law enforcement career produces changes in the person. The job takes on more and more of the officer's time and becomes more than just a job—it can become the central and defining aspect of the officer's life. Without insight into what changes are taking place, the significant people in the officer's personal life can find themselves pushed aside, searching for a way to adapt to these changes or risk losing the relationship. Marriages are strained—some break. Children are all too often alienated from parental emotional support. The spouse or parent dimension of the new officer's life can become secondary to the cop dimension. The new officer can become emotionally distant, hardened, or physically absent from the lives of the people sharing the journey through the police career from the home front.

The job takes on more and more of the officer's time and becomes more than just a job—it can become the central and defining aspect of the officer's life.

These changes taking place in the new officer's life are often alluded to or spoken of in the police culture, but rarely, if ever, are these changes seen as a major priority to correct. Very rarely are the changes in a new officer's personal life seen as anything but inevitable. Recruits are told that the job takes its toll, but they are hardly ever told or shown how to minimize the negative effects of the journey through the police career. Helping officers keep their personal lives intact is not a priority for many law enforcement agencies. Typically, agencies give no strategies or preventive game plans to the recruit.

These changes are not a problem isolated to a few law enforcement officers. They affect many new officers and families. Evidence of these changes are apparent by looking around any law enforcement agency and seeing the wreckage, both personal and professional, affecting the lives of many officers and police families.

Ironically, these changes in the personal lives of the new police officers are directly related to the very mindset that keeps officers safe while doing their job in the field.

Emotional Changes Lead to Physical Changes

The changes in officers' lives are not limited to their emotions or worldview. The emotional changes take place first: Anger can become a prevailing and ever-present state in a police home. Then, as the years pass, physical changes can begin to appear. The constant anger and the physical upheaval it causes, combined with years of shift-work-induced sleep deprivation, poor diet, and a sedentary personal lifestyle, can lead the now veteran officer to face physical changes in addition to emotional issues. Physical fitness and positive recreation can deteriorate and disappear from officers' lives. The veteran officer can look back on the journey through the police career from a different perspective compared to the one she or he held as a new recruit years before. The veteran officer can form two conclusions. The first may be a retrospective assessment of the journey:

"If I had to do it all over again, I don't think I'd become a cop. I'd go into some other line of work."

The second conclusion of the veteran officer can take the form of a forward-looking formulation of long-off retirement plans:

"Ten more years and I'm the hell out of here."

The officer's journey, all too often, takes its toll—a toll in worldview and outlook from positive to negative, from idealistic to cynical, from physically active and fit to sedentary and potentially unhealthy.

The cost of the journey can be measured in many ways. Professionally, minor dissatisfaction with the organization or agency can become all-consuming anger, hostility, and open hatred toward the management hierarchy of the police agency. The cost, unfortunately, can also be tabulated personally in failed marriages, children in trouble, and life views dominated by negativity, social isolation, and alienation from fellow human beings.

The veteran officer retiring after twenty or more years of service may not even vaguely resemble the positive, committed, and highly motivated recruit who began the journey. The scars, both physically and emotionally, are all too often clearly visible. Considering the potential costs of a police career to the officers themselves, their families, and the public they serve, what can be done to change this journey? What causes the changes, and can something be done to prevent or reduce the negative impact and damage to the officers and their families?

Officer Survival

Taking into account the old adage "If it's predictable, it's preventable," why are the predictable emotional changes and difficulties in an officer's life not prevented? Why aren't law enforcement organizations at least attempting major efforts to prevent the destructive effects on employees brought on by years spent as officers? Although many agencies do have dedicated police psychologists and employee assistance programs available, these traditionally have been focused on resolving issues once they develop, not on preventing them. These mental health professionals are highly dedicated to helping "broken cops," but organizationally and professionally, it's far past time to stop breaking cops.

The law enforcement culture does, in fact, clearly value certain types of prevention and survival training. Any training that reduces and prevents physical injury and death

Street survival and officer safety training must be the number one training priority; however, officer safety does not have to be the only training priority.

to officers is highly valued. The focus of this training and preventive awareness, however, is on physical assault and injury. Keeping cops alive on the street is clearly the goal, which is understandable. After all, those injuries are visible, tangible, and immediate. Every police officer and those who care about police officers would agree that the development of professional skills in the area of officer safety is the most basic necessity. No one would argue against the need for significant investment of training resources in officer safety to maximize street survival skills. Attendance at any police memorial service shows how lethal police work can be and the price that agencies, communities, and, most important, families pay in terms of officers' lives. Unfortunately, the development of skills to survive the emotional aspects of a police career is given far less, if any, attention relative to the development of skills to survive the physical assaults of police work. Street survival and officer safety training must be the number one training priority; however, officer safety does not have to be the *only* training priority. The most important training skill given to an officer is the skill to come home every night after shift, but street survival skills demand that emotional survival skills also be taught.

Survival Training Works

The development of officer safety training as a legitimate area of expertise over the past decades has produced significant results and has saved many police officers' lives. This excellent survival training has resulted in significant reductions in the number of felonious line-of-duty deaths experienced by police officers. Although the number of officers policing the United States has grown significantly over the past four decades, the number of those officers dying feloniously continues to decline. This is the result of good cops practicing effective officer safety.

Despite being faced with increasing gang activity, readily available automatic weapons, and a court system imparting questionable consequences for criminal activity, police officers are surviving the streets. Making officer safety training a high priority, combined with advancements in technology and equipment, such as improved ballistic vests and communications systems and enhanced EMS response, have produced an increased chance of survival for officers confronting lethal threat. This form of training is accepted and valued in police culture. Officers take a personal sense of ownership and responsibility for the development of their officer safety skills while working in the street environment. The number one priority for street officers is "stay alive so you can go home after shift." The culture takes officer safety so seriously that cops will refuse to work with an officer who repeatedly practices poor officer safety. It is culturally the highest priority.

Law Enforcement Felony Deaths

Year	Deaths	Year	Deaths
• 1970	100	• 1996	61
• 1971	129	• 1997	70
• 1972	116	• 1998	61
• 1973	134	• 1999	42
• 1974	132	• 2000	51
• 1975	129	• 2001	70 (includes 9/11)
• 1976	111	• 2002	56
• 1977	93	• 2003	52
• 1978	93	• 2004	54
• 1979	106	• 2005	55
• 1980	104	• 2006	48
• 1981	91	• 2007	57
• 1982	92	• 2008	41
• 1983	80	• 2009	48
• 1984	72	• 2010	56
• 1985	78	• 2011	72
• 1986	66	• 2012	49
• 1987	74	• 2013	27
• 1988	78	• 2014	51
• 1989	66	• 2015	41
• 1990	66	• 2016	66
• 1991	71	• 2017	46
• 1992	64	• 2018	55
• 1993	70	• 2019	48
• 1994	79	• 2020	48
• 1995	74		

Source: "Homicide Trends in the United States," Bureau of Justice Statistics, https://www.bjs.gov/content/pub/pdf/htus8008.pdf; and "Officers Killed and Assaulted," Bureau of Justice Statistics, https://www.bjs.gov/index.cfm?ty=tp&tid=701.

Are Officers Really Surviving?

Officer safety training, no matter how essential and valid, does not have to be the only training priority. It does not need to be at the expense of training in the realities of the emotional effects of the career. Street survival training itself does not address the full picture of risk exposure for police officers. Although in many ways, officers are winning the battle of street survival, they appear to be fatally losing the battle of emotional survival. Increasing suicide rates among law enforcement ranks is stark evidence of the cost of a law enforcement career. One 2019 statistical analysis found the number of police deaths by suicide was twice the line-of-duty deaths. The study pointed out the 132 line-of-duty deaths compared with 228 officer suicides (Blue H.E.L.P. 2020, bluehelp.org). Although the exact numbers may vary across the many specific police suicide studies, the conclusions are identical. The

Although in many ways officers are winning the battle of street survival, they appear to be fatally losing the battle of emotional survival.

emotional toll of a law enforcement career is unacceptably high. It's not the purpose of this book to cite exact numbers of police suicides. One police suicide is one too many. The numerical difference between felony death and suicide, however, should raise significant concern among both police officers and agencies, but unfortunately this startling information often falls on deaf ears.

The loss of even one police officer's life to a felony is unacceptable in police culture. Police officers and agencies do everything within their combined power to increase officer survival. Training, equipment, and resources are dedicated to reducing felony death. Yet the suicide rate for police has often been ignored. Across the span of studies on the number of police suicides compared to line-of-duty deaths over past decades, there is little difference in the overall conclusions. Line-of-duty deaths for most decades have trended downward, and police suicides have trended upward.

There does not appear to be a systematic recognition by agencies or officers of the emotional toll of police work and its contributing effect on self-destructive behavior. Police suicide is the obvious example of a police officer's failure to survive emotionally, but more insidious "silent killers," such as chronic depression, obesity, substance abuse, heart disease, and type 2 diabetes, are also taking a large toll in the lives of dedicated cops.

The reports that indicate police officers have a significantly higher suicide rate than the general population is even more alarming when you consider that it is general practice in most police agencies to conduct preemployment psychological evaluations of potential officers to rule out the preexistence of psychological abnormalities before hiring. Considering the major efforts police agencies put into preemployment screening of police applicants, it should be reasonably safe to assume that officers begin their careers psychologically more stable, physically more fit, and with fewer ongoing significant emotional crises than the general population. Why does the law enforcement profession face such alarming reported rates of self-destruction?

But That Can't Happen to Us

Some officers will look at the reported rates of suicide among law enforcement and rationalize:

> *"That's big city cops. I work in a small town, and that kind of stuff doesn't happen here."*

That is denial hard at work attempting to make it easier on officers and agencies not to put the emotional survival of all personnel on the front burner. The Fraternal Order of Police (FOP) represents law enforcement professionals from agencies of all sizes. It represents nearly half the nation's law enforcement officers. It is the nation's largest police association, and it should be commended for its courage to take a hard look at the issue of suicide within its membership ranks at a time well before police suicide was even being discussed. Compared to the average U.S. suicide rate of 12 per 100,000 (as reported by the Centers for Disease Control and Prevention), the FOP found rates among officers that were alarmingly high: 22 per 100,000 officer members.

Suicide isn't the only form of self-destruction: Depression, social isolation, and chronic anger also lead to the destruction of many other aspects of officers' lives that are not so readily visible. The journey through the police career clearly takes its toll. Suicides are just the extreme tip of the iceberg of emotional damage. Unfortunately, even this most extreme measure of psychological despair can be denied and rationalized away by the average officer and agency:

"Too bad about Joe. He just let this job get to him."

"Not everybody is cut out to be a cop."

"You got to know when to get out of here before you start thinking of eating your gun."

"Don't ever let this job get you that messed up."

"I thought Pat had her head screwed on tighter than that."

"What was wrong with him to do something like that to his kids?"

These statements can be heard at police agencies after a friend or fellow officer has taken her or his life. The surviving coworkers' statements are designed to make sense out of what happened and to put a safe distance between themselves and the officer who has committed suicide. Suicide by a healthy fellow cop can represent an act that the officers many times do not understand.

"How did this happen?"

"Why did this happen?"

"Did we miss something?"

Officers will ask these questions again and again in the time immediately after a police suicide. As the immediate sense of loss and bereavement lessens for the cops, however, the questioning diminishes. Any personal or organizational changes to be made and possibly any lessons to be learned from the tragedy are usually lost as everyone returns to the fast-paced world of police calls to answer and services to provide.

Denial Can Be Deadly

After a fellow cop commits suicide, many officers have to develop strategies to avoid acknowledging the real emotional impact the job can have. Officers design techniques to blunt and deny the realities. This means putting emotional distance between what happened and the world the officer still works and resides in every day. To keep the suicide of a fellow officer at a safe emotional distance, fellow officers must tell themselves that the suicide must have been the result of some flaw in the individual psychological makeup of the dead officer:

"Something must have been going on in her life that none of us knew about."

"I thought Joe had it more together than that."

Keeping psychological distance between the events that lead to a fellow cop committing suicide and the events that affect the surviving cops is essential if the officers have to keep doing the job without any insight or strategy for emotional survival. Denial creates the belief that psychological distance exists between what was going on in the dead officer's life and what is going on in the lives of the remaining officers. This helps create an illusion that "I'm doing okay," and "that stuff doesn't apply to me." Basically, it is a primitive attempt to ignore the emotional changes caused by police work and to deny emotional vulnerability. It's an attempt to avoid acknowledging the darker side of police work, the downside of the job. Many times, the only acknowledged glimpse of the darker side of police work is this often-heard phrase:

"I started out my career loving it, but I am starting to hate it and count the time until I'm out of here."

Both officers and agencies can rationalize suicide as an isolated tragedy reflective only of the events existing in the life of the deceased officer. But what about the loss and deterioration of other aspects of the police officers' emotional lives, such as the destruction of functional intimate relationships, the loss of productive and loving parental roles in their children's lives, or just the loss of being happy on a daily basis? The realities of these day-to-day losses are harder to keep distance from than a suicide and can be seen without exception in any police agency. These losses are much closer to home and much harder to deny. The suicide rate of police officers, although terribly tragic, is not nearly as numerically significant as the number of marriages that are lost and the number of children who grow up emotionally distant from their police parents and, unfortunately, who grow up experiencing the secondhand effects of a police career. How many vibrant physically fit police recruits transition into lethargic obese individuals by the end of their police career?

Cynicism, anger, isolation, and social distrust affect too many police homes. When a police family is discussing the neighbors, who possibly have a different opinion on an issue, the idea of differences of opinions is not discussed. It's easier just to conclude, "The neighbors are assholes." For the police officer and police family, the world becomes "full of assholes." For most police officers, the concepts of social isolation and cynicism aren't a problem; they are just "the way the world really is."

> *"If a 747 airliner with approximately 300 passengers on board crashed each year, the Federal Aviation Administration would ground 747s until the problem was discovered and corrected, yet we lose 300 police officers every year to suicide and we think that is just the cost of doing business."*
>
> —Robert Douglas, National P.O.L.I.C.E. Suicide Foundation
> (quoted in G. Fields, "Suicide on the Force," *USA Today,* June 1, 1999, p. 1A)

The toll in suicides, lost families, and the lost emotional and physical well-being of the men and women who set their career goals as public service, "to serve and protect," is absolutely unacceptable. **Whose job is it to serve and protect the officers and their families from the emotional risks of the job?**

Are the Changes Inevitable?

3

Can the journey through a law enforcement career be made easier, safer, and less emotionally and physically damaging to the police officer? Is the young, idealistic police recruit forced to experience the deteriorating emotional and physical changes brought on by the job? Is the recruit destined to undergo these changes without exception or hope of emotional survival? Does the new police officer have any hope of remaining an emotionally stable, physically fit individual who enjoys both a fulfilling career in police work and a functional, healthy, and happy personal life?

Many police officers, in fact, do survive emotionally and remain functional, healthy individuals after twenty or thirty years of police work.

Many police officers, in fact, do survive emotionally and remain functional, healthy individuals after twenty or thirty years of police work. Many police families remain loving, functional, and supportive. These families can be seen interacting with members of the general community—at community events, activities at their place of worship, and sporting events. If some officers are able to remain emotionally functional, every police family and law enforcement agency needs to ask some questions:

- How do these folks survive the job emotionally?
- Is it anything besides just lucky breaks?
- Can the agency help other officers to also survive emotionally?
- Are police agencies making the emotional survival of their members an issue of highest priority?

- Are police unions and fraternal organizations addressing the issues of their membership's emotional well-being?

- Is emotional survival for law enforcement officers an ongoing point of professional discussion?

- How often are police officers permitted to review, through targeted training, the impact of the job on issues such as anger, racism, happiness, depression, substance abuse, and overall physical health?

The Role of Organizations in Emotional Survival

Although most agencies and unions have counseling services available for personnel *after* problems surface, typically neither police agencies nor unions make the emotional well-being of their officers a high priority from a prevention perspective. This can become evident when some high-profile event occurs in the community that throws the agency into a controversy. The events causing the controversy at a police agency many times relate to the behavior of some of its officers. For example, a controversy surfaces pertaining to an allegation of officer misconduct: This could be an abusive-use-of-force complaint, a racial incident, an integrity issue, or possibly a tragedy revolving around domestic violence in a police family. The media picks up the controversy and reports the events, obviously using whatever spin best serves the needs of the media. Bad news sells and gets airtime. Now, however, in light of the controversy, questions do get asked of the police agency about what services are available for its law enforcement personnel:

- Are your officers psychologically screened before you give them guns?

- Do your officers have counseling available to them if they have a personal problem?

- Is there a substance abuse program available for department members to use?

- Do your officers receive ongoing training in police ethics?

Defensive Reactions instead of Constructive Actions

The questions come from the media, politicians, and the community. Sometimes the questions come fast and furiously. The media, after some highly publicized incident, can be seen at first as holding the police agency's feet to the fire regarding the psychological well-being of its officers. Initially, the media questioning appears to be a genuine effort to produce change, a desire to obtain assistance for the officers and to produce and demand change in the way officers conduct business, how the officers treat the public, how they treat the minority community, or how they report or fail to report the evidence of wrongdoing by fellow police officers. At first brush, it appears these media and community inquiries might produce some benefit for the agency and the officers themselves. Maybe some changes will be implemented that will make the journey through a police career easier. Maybe better psychological and counseling services will be provided.

The media, however, typically reports from a fundamentally antipolice perspective. "Vilify the cops" is always a good strategy to sell papers. The inherent antipolice media perspective on most controversies revolving around police officers' behavior does not typically cause officers to step back and review how they are doing emotionally. Usually, the media reports do little more than cause the rank-and-file officers, as well as management, to circle the wagons and take a defensive perspective, reinforcing the idea in most officers' minds that

"The media really are a bunch of bleeding-heart assholes."

"People in the community don't have any idea what working on the streets as a cop is really all about."

Missed Opportunities

Sometimes the crisis becomes a missed opportunity for labor and management to form a necessary partnership to enhance the help that could be available for officers and their families. On occasion, when a highly publicized incident occurs at a law enforcement agency, some elements of the organized rank and file of that agency can attempt to exploit the crisis or controversy to generate political fallout against the incumbent agency management, a payback for past labor-management disputes. Some more aggressive labor leaders consider the crisis a great opportunity to initiate a vote of "no confidence" against the chief. This is when the shouts can be heard:

"If it happened on the chief's watch, the chief should be held accountable."

It sounds good, but is this attitude really producing changes in how police officers will survive their careers emotionally? Does it really get more help or support for the officer's emotional well-being? Fortunately, some labor organizations see the situation and accurately and sincerely mobilize their resources to demand enhanced mental health services for their memberships.

The agency's higher-level management, when faced with a controversy concerning officer behavior or misconduct, will attempt to show the community that the "chief is addressing the issue"; however, just like the officers, the administration often takes a defensive position. The posture might look different, but the response is equally defensive, particularly if high-ranking department personnel are part of the controversy through either action or inaction.

"We are presently conducting an investigation of the alleged behavior of the officers in question, all of whom presently have been placed on administrative leave pending the outcome of the investigation."

Obviously, this position may clearly represent a necessary and genuine organizational attempt to increase accountability for its officers. Yet, even if genuine management action is taken concerning the controversial behavior of the officers, it usually represents a disciplinary reaction to the problem and fails to address correction *and* prevention. The agency deals with the symptoms but doesn't address the root causes of the problem. When controversies concerning officer behavior erupt, they typically indicate that an officer or group of officers has failed to survive the job emotionally. Unfortunately, both labor and management miss the opportunity to turn a negative experience into a positive outcome by assisting the officers. Inappropriate behavior erupts, and both labor and management jointly fail to address the big picture. No one benefits from the emotional and behavioral devastation and crisis in the lives of police officers. The agency, the individual officers and their families, and the entire community experience a loss.

When controversies concerning officer behavior erupt, they typically indicate that an officer or group of officers has failed to survive the job emotionally.

On so many occasions, labor and management fail to form joint partnerships of mutual benefit to all the stakeholders involved and ask the questions that are in the mutual interest of all parties:

- Why did this happen?

- How do we make the journey through the career easier and more balanced emotionally for our officers?

- Was this entire crisis avoidable?

- Can some basic change in the emotional preparation and maintenance of law enforcement officers take place?

- Can we teach police officers to be emotional survivors, the types of officers who make it through a career remaining highly productive and effective as cops, yet having balanced and effective personal lives? Can the journey be made easier?

What Is Actually Taking Place?

Before we can initiate assistance for law enforcement officers, we need to know exactly what changes an officer goes through. The best way to find out what changes affect police officers is to go straight to the source—ask the cops themselves:

- "Do you see the world differently now that you are an officer?"
- "Do you look at people differently?"
- "Do you read situations differently?"

Experienced police officers answer each of these questions with a resounding "Yes."

- "Yes, I see people differently."
- "You bet I look at things from a different perspective now that I am a cop."
- "Yes, I see things now I never saw before or even knew existed before I became a cop."

A Matter of Perspective

Most officers realize that they see the world differently but have never stopped to assess just how differently they perceive things. They typically don't have time to worry about it. The people they spend most

> The people they spend most of their time with see the world pretty much the same way they do—these people, of course, are other cops.

23

of their time with see the world pretty much the same way they do—these people, of course, are other cops. The need for officers to step back and look at changes in their worldviews since becoming officers appears to be a total waste of time, absolute nonsense, little more than touchy-feely garbage. Real changes, however, have taken place.

Has Your Worldview Changed?

The following word-association exercise will help you become aware of changes in your outlook since becoming an officer. Don't worry: This test doesn't require anything psychologically abstract like looking at inkblots. It involves simply looking at the word that appears below and saying the first thing that comes to your mind.

scout leader

What was the first word that came to your mind? Did you say something like "pedophile," "child molester," or "sex offender"?

The vast majority of times officers take the above word-association test, their responses are negative evaluations of the term *scout leader*. Most people, however, see this term in a positive light. When I try this word-association test on other groups of adults, such as service club members, I get a different set of responses. Typically, the nonpolice groups respond to the term *scout leader* with something like the following answer:

"An adult man or woman interested in helping youth, primarily through outdoor activities."

I have tested a large number of law enforcement groups and have never received that positive response from officers. When I point out that their response is unique, some officers become defensive:

"Don't tell me it's some way that I see the world. I don't know where you live, but let me tell you about the real world—it's the way the world is, not how I see it—it's how it is. Every scout leader I have ever met has been a pedophile. Normal adults don't wear shorts and take groups of little boys hiking in the woods."

Before condemning the officer as incorrect, it is important to review his response: "Every scout leader I have ever met has been a pedophile." He's probably exactly right. Every scout leader he has ever met has been a pedophile—odds are, so has every teacher he's ever met, every truck driver, or even every astronaut. He's a cop, in this case a sex-crimes detective—he doesn't meet normal people. He knows victims, and he knows suspects. He is probably a subject matter expert in the law enforcement area of sex crimes. He knows a great deal about investigating sex crimes. He knows how to control a crime scene, preserve evidence, take statements, and prepare a case for presentation to the prosecutor to have the case issued and a warrant obtained. He knows his area of expertise. In terms of the whole world, however, how wide an area does the subject matter involved in sex crimes really cover? It represents a very narrow slice of the world. After a while, that narrow slice of the world, known as police work, can become the officer's entire worldview. The view is typically one of negativity, anger, violence, and trauma. Police officers have lots of data from which to draw conclusions about the world; however, as the years go by, because of the world the officers are immersed in, the data become more and more contaminated and so do the conclusions the officers draw.

Cynicism

Law enforcement personnel, like all human beings, form their worldviews and predictions about life from the situations and events they see every day. Who calls the police to their home because things are going well? Can you imagine a law enforcement dispatcher receiving the following telephone call for service from a citizen?

"Hello, police department? I just got home, and I discovered the house is really clean, and my spouse made a great meal for us, and the kids all made the honor roll at school, and we are even a little ahead financially. Please send some officers—and hurry!"

Even the thought of receiving such a call is ludicrous. People call law enforcement when things are not working out, not when things are going well. It has been said that officers see people at their maddest, baddest, and saddest. Is it any wonder that the officers' worldviews change?

> Law enforcement personnel, like all human beings, form their worldviews and predictions about life from the situations and events they see every day. Who calls the police to their home because things are going well?

Try the scout-leader test on even some sub-specialties of law enforcement officers, such as National Park Service Rangers and Bureau of Land Management Rangers. These are the men and women who provide law enforcement services on public lands. They are as much law enforcement officers as their city or county counterparts; the only difference is that the few thousand people a day who visit their "city" (the park or public recreation area) change each day. Ask Rangers what comes to mind when they hear the term *scout leader* and the response many times is some offshoot of the following:

"An incompetent adult who marches youth to their deaths!"

What is taking place in the minds of these men and women that causes them to see things so differently from the average person? *Scout leader* for most people invokes an image of a caring and trustworthy adult. Why isn't this the case in the minds of our law enforcement officers? Could it be the type of contact law enforcement officers have with a small number of scout leaders that shapes their entire worldview? Could the answer lie in the fact that police work makes people cynical?

Cynical: Contemptuously distrustful of human nature and motive.
—Webster's Collegiate Dictionary

Think for a moment of the world of the street police officer. Does being distrustful of human nature and motive have a purpose? Yes, it keeps cops alive. It is highly essential that every police officer—making every call for service, making every traffic stop—practice excellent officer safety skills, which translates into being distrustful. Officers don't know which traffic stop is going to culminate in an officer-involved shooting, so they must be distrustful of human nature and motive at each and every traffic stop and at *all* calls for service. This is common sense to the experienced police officer. What happens, however, when the distrust does not remain just an occupational observational skill set that the officer has honed while working the street? What happens when the officer sees everything and everybody through the same filter of distrust? What happens when the officer's worldview is one of distrust? The officer arriving at this point is cynical. It's a mindset that works well on the street but wreaks havoc on one's personal life. No one is trusted, except, obviously, a few select cops.

> *Does being distrustful of human nature and motive have a purpose? Yes, it keeps cops alive.*

"Everybody has an angle."

"Don't be naive. He's not as nice as you think he is."

This type of cynical outlook projects negativity into activities and social gatherings and can be extremely difficult on nonpolice friends and members of the officer's family. The officer can be viewed as negative, distrusting, hard, and unforgiving.

Ask police officers if they are cynical and most will respond:

*"You bet I'm cynical. You would be too if you saw half
the stuff I see every day at work."*

Ask officers' significant others if the officers have become cynical, and you might get an answer similar to the following comment.

*"My husband and I were on vacation recently with my
parents. We were driving through a city about 100
miles from our home. My father was in the front seat
with my husband, and my mother and I were in the
back seat. My mother notices a teenage boy riding a
new bicycle and she comments, 'Look, that boy has
a nice bike,' to which my husband responds, 'Yeah,
that means someone else doesn't have their nice bike
anymore.' I ask my husband, 'Do you always have to be
so negative?' and he says, 'Honey, I'm just telling it like
it is.'"*

—an officer's wife

When asked, officers admit to being cynical, but many times
they are not aware of the long-term impact cynicism creates on
attempting to maintain a normal social, family, and emotional life.
There is a high cost to one's personal life by being cynical. The cost
can be seen in how law enforcement officers view life in general.
Although not recognized by the officer, cynicism also plays a potential long-term role in the development of obesity, heart disease,
and type 2 diabetes.

The Cynicism Ratio

If you want to determine if you have become cynical, take this simple test of your individual cynicism ratio. The cynicism ratio will show numerically to what degree cynicism has invaded your worldview. To take the cynicism test, perform the following mathematical calculation:

Take the square root of the number of times you say "bullshit" on an average day.

Using the above equation, many officers would see both themselves and their fellow officers score highly on the cynicism scale each day. Any time something occurs that they disagree with, "it's bullshit." A memo arrives down the chain of command from the administration, and before they even read it, officers respond with a chorus of

"Look at this bullshit. Don't they have anything better to do than micromanage the troops?"

"I wish they would just let you do the job and quit dumping bullshit on you."

"Did you read that memo from the chief?" "I don't read that bullshit. Give the chief a week and there will be another bullshit memo saying the total opposite. It's just all bullshit."

As the years in a police career pass, anything and everything an officer disagrees with, doesn't like, or finds different is "bullshit." It comes in many varieties:

- political bullshit
- administrative bullshit
- affirmative action bullshit
- management bullshit (for union members only)
- union bullshit (for management only)
- touchy-feely bullshit
- total bullshit

The list could go on and on. It represents officers' anger, frustration, and growing intolerance of things that bombard them every day while doing their jobs as police officers. This can be observed daily at any law enforcement agency by listening to officers chant their daily mantra:

"Being a cop wouldn't be so bad if it weren't for all the bullshit."

The frustration and overwhelming need to turn it all off causes the officer to take a psychological shortcut by just labeling things "bullshit." It beats having to listen to people's problems every day at work—the same problems the officer has been listening to for the past five or ten years and probably will be listening to for the next ten or fifteen years. It's just easier to shut down psychologically and distance yourself from the events around you. Officers can put up protective shields and not be affected by the events around them. They don't have to think about things they disagree with. They just label them "bullshit" and move on.

Officers don't have to try to explain or deal with events outside their comfort zone. Creating this distance is a much less painful way of facing the emotional challenges of police work in the short run.

Officers don't have to try to explain or deal with events outside their comfort zone. Creating this distance is a much less painful way of facing the emotional challenges of police work in the short run. Saying, "It's just bullshit anyway; don't worry about it," however, is not an effective tactic in the long run for learning the skills to survive emotionally as a police officer or to effectively do the demanding job of handling interpersonal conflict required of police officers. What happens to young enthusiastic and idealistic men and women when they begin thinking everything is bullshit? How long before the core values and idealism they brought to the job begin eroding and start seeming like meaningless, useless, and extremely naive ways of viewing the world that police officers see every day? And how long before this belief spreads to the remaining areas of an officer's life?

The Source of All the Bullshit

As cynicism develops, and everything becomes bullshit, the officer has to be able to explain the source:

Where does all this bullshit come from? Who causes all this bullshit?

Soon an obvious answer appears. Every officer knows who causes all the bullshit:

The assholes.

Now the police officer, who is growing in both street experience and, simultaneously, cynicism, can explain any social dilemma or problem that presents itself:

"It's just bullshit, and this guy is an asshole."

Now there is no longer any need to deal with the problems officers encounter every day. They just go through the motions because "it's just bullshit anyway." Anyone they don't agree with "is just an asshole." All "alternative life forms" are assholes. That means that anyone officers don't like, don't trust, are uncomfortable with, or don't even know is an asshole. The longer someone is a law enforcement officer, the larger the number of assholes he or she knows. Fewer and fewer people in the officer's life are spared the label. By the time many officers are ready for retirement, they can count on one hand the number of people who are *not* assholes. Also, the more years someone is an officer, the more different varieties of assholes, or "proctological personalities," the officer discovers or creates. Because the term is reserved for anyone the officer doesn't trust, and many cops trust no one but a small inner circle of partners and friends, the world soon appears overpopulated with assholes.

To keep the different varieties of assholes straight, officers many times creatively generate subtypes:

- known assholes

- flaming assholes

- management assholes (for use by union members only)

- union assholes (for use by management only)

- federal assholes (for use by local and state cops only)

- local assholes (for use by federal agents only)

- political assholes (for use by everyone in law enforcement)

The only thing limiting the creation of new categories is the imagination of the cops involved, but remember—cops can be very creative. What the term *asshole* really designates, for an officer, is an individual who causes the officer to experience a state of physical uneasiness or discomfort. This state of physical discomfort lets the officer know he or she is in potential jeopardy when this person, the asshole, is present. The jeopardy could be physical risk, occupational risk, or emotional risk. Early on in a police officer's career, the feeling of jeopardy is usually experienced only in street encounters, where physical risk occurs. The essence of street survival for police officers is the ability to appreciate the feeling of being in jeopardy in most situations and to use that feeling to mobilize enhanced street survival skills. Feeling in jeopardy permits the officer to be prepared in case something potentially threatening occurs. This is the street survival mindset.

Social Perception Test

Many experienced police officers would find it virtually impossible to travel around their jurisdiction for thirty minutes and not see at least one asshole. The job of being a cop has turned them into Mobile Proctology Detection Units. They drive around their beat and locate assholes and hopefully intervene before the identified Adam Henry engages in their assholeish behavior. For many good cops, this outgrowth of the perceptual set, or way of viewing the world, required for practicing officer safety changes their lives. If there were one hundred people standing across the street from a good street cop, and one person in the crowd was a "card-carrying asshole," that person would probably stand out to the cop as though he or she were waving a flag. A good cop can spot an asshole in a herd.

The drawback of this heightened selective perception is that the cop no longer sees the herd. So the one person in the group is readily perceived by the cop, but ninety-nine others go unnoticed. The cop begins going through life on 1 percent of the data, ignoring the other 99 percent. This effect on the officer's perception is actually based in the neurological foundation of survival.

Most officers are familiar with or have heard of the concept of *auditory blockage*, where during officer-involved shootings, officers report not hearing their weapons being discharged. At the range while firing their weapon in a basically safe environment, the booming sound of the weapon requires wearing ear protection. On the street in a life-or-death situation, however, officers many times report hearing only a slight muffled sound or no sound at all when their weapons fire. All sensory processes are intensely focused on the relevant threat. The sound of the weapon discharging is irrelevant and does not register, hence the term auditory blockage. On the street, once the officer focuses in on the one asshole in the herd, the ninety-nine other "normal" folks become irrelevant.

"Every scout leader I've ever met has been a pedophile."

Probably an absolutely truthful statement, but how many scout leaders have officers actually met outside their professional law enforcement role?

As the years pass, officers becomes quite competent in their street survival skills, but this perceptual set based on the feeling of potential jeopardy becomes pervasive in officers' worldviews. It soon begins affecting the perception of people within the police agency hierarchy, hence the often-heard statement:

> *"I can handle the assholes on the street. I just can't handle the assholes running this agency."*

It really means, "I have good street survival skills, but I feel far more threatened by the people in management."

Taking Cynicism Home

Now, armed with these two concepts, the officer can be protected from the emotional battering experienced every day at work. They are effective concepts if the officer's goal is to blunt feelings, avoid getting hurt, and function in a hostile world of negative experiences. But is the officer's entire world really full of negative experiences? What about at home?

How does this social alienation and cynicism affect the personal life of the officer? How does the officer who has not been given information or guidance on dealing with cynicism learn to live a balanced life? What happens when the officer's

> *How often do officers let their anger and cynicism cloud their judgment, even in the way they speak to their children and families?*

eight-year-old son wants to join the Boy Scouts? How does the officer let the boy join an organization if she or he believes that all scout leaders are pedophiles? How does the cynical police officer function as a parent?

The following dialogue between parent and child demonstrates the impact of cynicism.

Child: *When we bought our pickup truck, you said Fords are the best pickup trucks.*

Parent: *That's right.*

Child: *Well, Johnny Jones down the street, his mom and dad just bought a new truck, and they said Chevys are the best pickup trucks.*

Now the parent has to take the time and energy to help shape the worldview of his or her child, to teach about differences of opinion and how to interact with people who think differently than the officer and his or her family think. Two basic response patterns are available in this straightforward parent-child interaction.

Parenting Response Option 1:
"Son, not everybody will agree with our opinions. Personally, we prefer Fords, but not everybody will prefer them. They have the right to believe differently than we do. We don't have to agree with them, but we have to respect their right to hold different opinions."

Parenting Response Option 2:
"Son, that's bullshit. Fords are much better trucks than Chevys. I think the Joneses are assholes, and I don't want you going down there to play anymore."

Obviously, Parent Response Option 1 takes a lot more energy and willingness to engage the child in learning to appreciate and accept differences. How often would the cynical, tired, and angry police officer, without thinking, opt for Parent Response Option 2?

How often do officers let their anger and cynicism cloud their judgment, even in the way they speak to their children and families? Unfortunately, many law enforcement parents, without thinking, let their cynicism and social isolation dictate the very manner in which they admonish their own children:

"Quit acting like a little asshole!"

"If you don't straighten up, you're going to grow up to be an asshole!"

Not exactly Mr. Rogers' Neighborhood, but then again, unfortunately, many cops would probably think Mr. Rogers was an asshole.

Is Cynicism Unavoidable?

Is it a forgone conclusion that cops are cynical individuals who think most people are assholes? Is it unavoidable that police officers will believe the answer to most social dilemmas or questions is "who cares, it's just bullshit anyway"? Must this happen? Absolutely not! Without effective training in emotional survival skills, however, both in the beginning of and throughout a law enforcement career, a cynical outlook is unfortunately the predictable result. Without taking time to make emotional survival a priority, many police officers' lives will be typified by a lifetime of cynicism-based thinking and decisions. The consequences of this type of thinking and interaction with children and loved ones are typically felt only years later in terms of failed love relationships and strained, or even broken, parent-child relationships that may never recover.

Where does this cynicism come from? Cynicism is actually the long-term outgrowth of a very necessary decision-making strategy that effective law enforcement professionals need to apply daily when on duty. It's a necessary element in a survival worldview in law enforcement. Cops by definition are called into situations to solve problems—all types of problems, things the average person can't or won't handle. If folks could handle the situations themselves, they probably wouldn't call law enforcement to begin with. From car accidents, noise complaints, domestic disputes, gun calls, barking dogs and anything else imaginable to, on many occasions, things that just aren't imaginable to the normal person, cops walk into unknowns and must figure things out. They have to figure them out rapidly and not lose their life in the learning process. They must be *street survivors.* Every call for service is a question mark for the cop to figure out. The cop is always walking into an unknown.

?

Normal decision-making processes do not work in the world of law enforcement. The very necessary and effective way good cops approach the *?* and problem solve lays the cynicism foundation. This in turn potentially creates much of the long-term destruction the officer experiences in his or her personal life. Lots of people in lots of jobs must solve lots of problems every day. They also have to figure out *?* It's just that cops are required to approach a problem from a 180-degree different approach then "normal" people. Most folks have the luxury of approaching a *?* by utilizing normal thinking. Let's call "normal" thinking *probability thinking.*

- How long is it *probably* going to take me to drive to that location?

- Dinner will be ready *probably* in twenty minutes.

- I think I'll buy that particular item because it looks like it is *probably* the best choice.

We often make our decisions either by ourselves or seeking guidance or input from others on what is *probably* the best course of action in our decision-making process. This type of normal thinking works well for most folks. But this normal thinking is a disaster when a law enforcement professional uses it.

> *"I'm not going to wear my body armor tonight because I'm probably not going to get shot."*
>
> *"I'm not going to take my duty weapon with me because I'm probably not going to need to shoot anyone today."*
>
> *"I can just approach that car in this traffic stop in any haphazard manner because there's probably not a weapon in the vehicle."*

The foundation for creating the inverse thinking that law enforcement is required to utilize lies in the cost of an incorrect calculation. For example:

Assumption: *It will probably take us twenty minutes to drive downtown.*

Reality: A major traffic disruption causes the trip to take forty-five minutes.

Cost of the probability error: twenty-five minutes of delay

Assumption: *There's probably not a gun in the car.*

Reality: There is a gun in the car.

Cost of the probability error: possibly the officer's life.

Police officers do not problem solve with probability thinking. Police officers problem solve with *possibility thinking*. Cops are required to view every situation from a worst-case scenario perspective and have a course of action to prevent the negative outcome from taking place. Possibility thinking requires officers to scan all the unknowns in a given situation and adjust their actions to reduce the threat. Possibility thinking becomes the order of the day for the law enforcement professional.

Possibility thinking requires:

- Wearing ballistic body armor
- Stepping to the side after knocking on a door
- Standing in the tactically superior position on a traffic stop

Possibility thinking is just another phrase for officer safety or street survival. It requires cops to always be seeing the worst possibility in any given situation or person they encounter. It saves lives in the short term, but without understanding, training, and intervention to undo what is taking place in the officer's worldview, it destroys lives in the long run. It is mandatory that cops master and implement possibility thinking, aka officer safety, every day, but it is the foundation for the psychological and physiological changes the law enforcement professional undergoes. Not only do officers have to see the world through the negative filter of all potentially threatening outcomes, but they have to do it with elevated alertness. Cops become hypervigilant.

Hypervigilance

5

What causes the psychological and physiological changes in law enforcement personnel? Is the negative, cynical, angry outlook that typifies many law enforcement officers directly related to and caused by the many tragic, negative, and violent events that an officer is forced to witness over the years of being a cop? Or is there something else occurring that affects the way law enforcement officers view the world?

Is it *what* cops see in the world? Or Is it *how* cops must learn to see the world? Is there a unique perceptual set, or way of viewing the world, that officers learn? Do law enforcement officers need to see the world differently than most folks? Do they need to learn to see the world as potentially lethal to be safe as cops? Of course. Officers *must* learn to see the world differently than most folks to increase the odds of going home each day after work.

> *Officers are exposed every day to a series of unknown events, any one of which could be perfectly harmless or lethally dangerous.*

> *"If I see the world as potentially violent, I'll be prepared for violence if it does take place."*

From the first day of academy training, through an entire career of police work, officers must learn to perceive the world as potentially hazardous in order to survive the streets. Officers are exposed every day to a series of unknown events, any one of which could be perfectly harmless or lethally dangerous. Officers have to guess which event is safe and which event is lethal. An officer can make

41

10,000 traffic stops and 9,999 are perfectly safe; however, one can take his or her life—the officer just doesn't know which specific one is lethal, and therefore must approach all 10,000 as potentially lethal. An officer making a traffic stop may be dealing with a family out for a drive or a fugitive with outstanding felony warrants. The officer must figure out which is the case by reading unknowns.

An old street adage states, "Bad guys don't wear name tags." Deciding which unknowns are harmless and which ones will prove to be lethal can be accomplished only by assuming that all the unknowns are *potentially* lethal unknowns until proved otherwise. An unknown situation can be proved harmless only after the fact. Officers reduce lethal threat by practicing this perceptual skill set known as *officer safety*. All situations are potentially lethal and require possibility thinking until proved otherwise.

Central to the development of any officer safety skills is the understanding that officers not only must perceive the environment as potentially lethal, but also must accomplish this perceptual task immediately, when time is of the utmost essence. They must perceive the environment rapidly and accurately. Interpreting each unknown as potentially lethal permits the officer to have a greater sense of preparedness, regardless of how the unknown event actually plays out in the end.

Better Safe than Sorry

In any situation, an officer can misread unknowns and miss lethal warning cues. What starts out as something harmless or routine can cost officers their lives.

"Is that person reaching for his wallet or a weapon?"

Not accepting the potential risk in any situation is not practicing good officer safety. Not being perceptive of every nuance of the environment can prove lethal. It is better to approach a harmless situation prepared for risk than to approach the lethal situation unprepared. Experienced police officers know that it is important to err on the side of perceptual preparedness rather than perceptual laziness.

This is absolute common sense to experienced street officers. They learn it early in their career, and officers don't want to work the streets with someone who doesn't see the world from

> Hypervigilance is the necessary manner of viewing the world from a threat-based perspective, having the mindset to see the events unfolding as potentially hazardous.

this cautious perspective. Officers will quickly comment on another officer's lack of street safety:

> *"They are just not safe to work with. Maybe they would be okay at a desk job, but not on the street. They are going to get someone hurt or killed."*

This perceptual set of elevated alertness to surroundings, which is required of law enforcement officers for survival, is referred to in police culture as officer safety; however, a more accurate term would be **hypervigilance.**

Hypervigilance is the necessary manner of viewing the world from a threat-based perspective, having the mindset to see the events unfolding as potentially hazardous. The effective and safe street officer must believe that every encounter possesses the potential of lethal risk. The perceptual set of hypervigilance lets the officer have an increased awareness of all the data available in the environment. As an officer makes a "routine" traffic stop, he or she needs to interpret the environment rapidly and accurately, asking the basic questions that reflect hypervigilance:

- Who is in the backseat?
- Where are everyone's hands?
- Where do I stand?
- Where do I move if this traffic stop goes bad and I have to defend myself?

Asking these questions is the necessary thought process of every effective law enforcement officer working in a street or risk environment. This is the essence of worst-case scenario thinking.

This perceptual set, which is required of effective police officers, has social, psychological, and—the most often ignored in police training—biological dimensions. The brain of the competent street police officer perceives the world from a perspective of hypervigilance. Rapid perception, quick interpretation of events, perceiving unknowns as potentially lethal until proved otherwise—these are all part of the hypervigilance mindset. The most important thing law enforcement officers do *every day* is go home to their loved ones after work *every day*. There is no such thing as too much officer safety. Learning to understand and deal with the long-term effects of necessary officer safety proves problematic for far too many good police officers.

Effects of Hypervigilance

How does this perceptual set of hypervigilance affect the officer psychologically and physiologically over a significant course of time? In the short run, during the early years of a police career, it is a fun, exciting, stimulating mindset. Watching the enthusiasm displayed or listening to newly minted cops, one often hears:

"Man, I love this job!"

"I can't believe they're paying me to do this. I'd do it for free."

"Being a cop is the most fun I've had with my clothes on."

This short-lived phase of the law enforcement career raises some questions that need to be understood and answered for the officer:

- What about as the years go by?
- What are the long-term effects?
- Does hypervigilance have effects on the officer's professional role?
- What are the effects of hypervigilance on the officer's personal life?
- What are the effects of hypervigilance on the officer's long-term physical wellness?

Can this hypervigilance perceptual set, that is so important for street survival, be the major contributing factor to the significant change emotionally and physically affecting many police officers across the span of their law enforcement careers? Could the perceptual set of hypervigilance, with its psychological and physiological dimensions, which are absolutely required for officer safety, be the catalyst in later years for depression, substance abuse, and even obesity, with its syndromes of elevated health risks?

Hypervigilance permits the on-duty officer to develop the perceptual set of worst-case scenario possibility thinking required for maximum officer safety. Every decision the officer makes is dependent on the perceptual set of hypervigilance. Each of the officer's decisions on an event such as a traffic stop demonstrates the impact of hypervigilance on behavior. Each action the officer takes is controlled by the perceptual set of hypervigilance: positioning and movements, how close he or she permits the citizen to stand, requesting and then requiring the citizen on a traffic stop to step away from a vehicle or to step away from a potential weapon or item of threat. This perceptual set soon becomes the officer's way of perceiving the world. When describing effective law enforcement officers who practice hypervigilance, one could say:

"Good officers learn to see the world as one big felony in progress. They are just driving through it, and they don't want any of it to splash on them."

This very necessary perceptual set of hypervigilance should be ever present in effective and safe law enforcement officers. It permits them to lower the potential risks to which they are exposed. Most people outside police work do not need to develop a perceptual set of hypervigilance. The average citizen encounters a normal level of daily risk. Most people have the luxury of "living between the lines," living within the normal range of emotion, risk, and reactivity to the environment. Living in the normal range of vigilance is a perfectly acceptable range for the average person dealing with a normal level of risk, threat, or demand. No need for most women and men to see the world as potentially threatening—if something goes wrong, they can just call the cops. Dial 911, and a first responder professional will resolve the issue. The average person can quite comfortably approach life "between the lines," as shown in the figure below:

Normal Range of Risk

Average citizens can live in the normal range of risk—between the lines—usually without consequence. They can see the world as a basically safe and positive place. Seeing the world as generally safe, rational, predictable, and fair are the foundations of a mentally healthy life. Cops learn early in their career that in their world, things are not safe, rational, predictable, and fair. The average person does not need to experience hypervigilance every day. One might experience it on a rare occasion—for example, walking down an unknown dark street in a bad neighborhood at night might permit the average citizen to experience hypervigilance. The unknown dark street presents many unknowns to the citizen. The average person might then begin asking the hypervigilance questions:

- Am I in harm's way?
- Is that person approaching me a potential assailant?
- Is that group of men following me?
- What is that sound I hear behind me?

All these questions are the evidence of the existence of a hypervigilant perceptual set.

"Let me pay attention to every sight, sound, and other sensory input available to increase my awareness of the environment and thus lower my chances of being victimized by an unknown."

The average citizen, during his or her daily routine, rarely experiences hypervigilance. It's an isolated situational event. When a situation does develop that exposes citizens to some potential risk in their environment, they often interpret the sensations as alertness, anxiety, or fear. The police officer experiences hypervigilance daily (or *should* experience it daily) if he or she is practicing good officer safety. It is the perceptual set that lets the officer see threat or risk before it takes its toll. Hypervigilance is what permits officers to survive the risks they encounter in the field. It is also, if unaddressed or ignored, what lays down the foundation of potential destruction in the officer's life professionally, personally, and physically.

The Biology of Hypervigilance

What exactly is hypervigilance and how does it affect officers? Hypervigilance is a biological state. Its foundation is in the neurological functioning of the brain. The brain has a set of structures, known as the *reticular activating system (RAS)*, that determine the level of alertness necessary at any given time. Whenever the brain interprets the existence of a potential for threat or risk, the RAS engages the higher-functioning levels of the brain into a higher level of awareness and perceptiveness of the environment. This response is meant to increase survival by enabling the brain to perceive potential threats before they take place. The increased level of alertness and awareness of the surrounding environment needed for officers to safely work the streets is caused by the hypervigilance response and produces an increased functioning of the sympathetic branch of the autonomic nervous system.

The *autonomic nervous system* controls the body's internal organs and automatic functions:

- pulse
- respiration
- body temperature
- blood pressure
- blood glucose
- and other functions

The level and pattern of responsiveness of the autonomic nervous system is an individual's characteristic manner of emotional reactivity to risk, demand, or threat. It is the person's basic physical level of reactivity to the environment, or the person's *physical temperament*. The autonomic nervous system is the biological aspect of the officer's sixth sense on the street—that capacity to be ready when something takes place or needs an immediate reaction, a reaction that just might keep the officer alive in a tough situation.

This state of alert interaction with the environment, at mild to moderate levels, is not unpleasant to experience physically.

The autonomic nervous system is divided into two separate and opposite branches, the *sympathetic* and *parasympathetic* branches. The sympathetic branch is the part of the autonomic nervous system that reacts and controls bodily function in times of challenge or threat. This is the branch that is involved during the police officer's day-to-day functioning. It could be considered the "on-duty" branch. During hypervigilance, the sympathetic branch turns on those bodily functions that are required for physical survival. This biological state of hypervigilance is the body's way of increasing survival through heightened functions:

- increased peripheral vision
- improved hearing
- faster reaction times
- increased blood glucose
- elevated heart rate
- increased blood pressure
- a general sense of energy to meet and overcome any threats that are challenging the body's capacity to survive

When on duty, the hypervigilant officer operates above the normal range of risk, as shown in the figure below.

Hypervigilance
On Duty

Alive, Alert, Energetic, Involved, Humorous

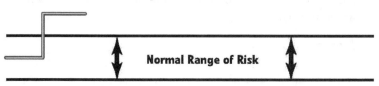

Unlike the civilian, who can live between the lines, the on-duty officer is above the line. The officer is practicing good officer safety, is experiencing hypervigilance, and has a perceptual set of preparedness for engaging in the environment to survive potential threats. Inattentiveness to the environment is lethal for on-duty police officers. Early in a law enforcement career, as officers are being introduced to on-duty police work, they make a conscious decision about their need for hypervigilance and its increased alertness concerning their surroundings. New officers can express this decision using varying words, but it usually takes the form of a thought like the following:

> *"I better pay attention out here. I could get killed, I could get hurt, I could get somebody else hurt."*

As mentioned above, the state of hypervigilance includes increased peripheral vision, more focused hearing, increased heart rate, elevated blood pressure, elevated blood glucose (sugar)—all biological responses that enhance survival.

The on-duty officer experiences this *objective biological state* as a subjective state of increased alertness, in-

Cops know what it feels like to be a cop. Just about everybody else is on the outside looking in.

creased awareness of the environment, elevated sense of attention, more rapid thinking, and increased capacity to make quick decisions and think on one's feet. While in a state of hypervigilance, officers also display good senses of humor—good but usually rather sick. This state of alert interaction with the environment, at mild to moderate levels, is not unpleasant to experience physically. In fact, it feels rather good physically—at least for the first few years of a law enforcement career.

"It's fun to be a cop."

This elevated level of the autonomic nervous system arousal (arousal of the sympathetic branch) makes people feel alive, quick witted, and able to handle any problems. Law enforcement officers experiencing hypervigilance interpret it as a unique feeling that comes about when they begin working on the streets or in any potentially threatening environment. Because the effective street police officer needs to believe all encounters are potentially threatening to increase his or her chances of survival, it only follows that the officer will experience this elevated sense of perceptual arousal, or hypervigilance, in almost all police-related encounters. Officers feel alive, involved, engaged—they feel a sense of camaraderie with those men and women who share the risk involved in police work. One of the reasons police relationships are quite intense and the culture close-knit is that the men and women of law enforcement know the feeling of hypervigilance, and it becomes the binding glue of police culture.

Cops know what it feels like to be a cop. Just about everybody else is on the outside looking in. The physical reactions and sensations of being a police officer are the defining parts of the culture. Other occupational cultures that frequently share intense or high-risk encounters also experience this close-knit cultural bonding. Firefighters, combat veterans, 911 operators, and EMS personnel all share the experience and the potential destruction hypervigilance can bring into their lives.

How Others Perceive Hypervigilance

The perceptual set of hypervigilance becomes inseparable from the police role. When an officer is engaged in a police-related activity, he or she experiences hypervigilance. People outside of police work observing hypervigilance often cannot understand why the officers acted the way they did during any given encounter. The citizen unaware of the concept of hypervigilance and the survival behaviors it will produce in the law enforcement officer can draw a totally inaccurate conclusion when viewing the officer's behavior.

"The officer seemed so rude. He didn't walk up to my car so I could get a good look at him next to the driver's door. He stood back behind the driver's door, so I had to turn way around just to look at him and talk to him. He seemed very serious and unfriendly."

How often during encounters with the police do citizens view the officer as rude, judging by behavior such as standing slightly behind the driver's door during a traffic stop? From the officer's perspective, this is good officer safety. He or she is dealing with an unknown (the citizen) from the worst-case scenario perspective of hypervigilance. The officer is watching every move the citizen makes to be able to react to any potential threat before it surfaces. Hypervigilance becomes the filter through which the law enforcement officer experiences the world. All situations are potentially lethal; all situations require attention, alertness, involvement, and quick intellectual assessment of the situation. All on-duty encounters require hypervigilance. The hypervigilant perceptual set is engaged not only while the officer is involved in an in-progress law enforcement encounter, but also whenever the officer is observing the world. It is the *potential* of risk for which the officer must be prepared—not the probability of risk but the possibility of risk. Citizens often misunderstand hypervigilance and the behavior it generates among police officers:

"Why did it take four cops to talk to the driver? He wasn't doing anything wrong."

This is a complaint from a citizen unaware of hypervigilance and how it necessarily drives officers' behavior. Citizens often cannot appreciate that the officers did not know that the driver wasn't going to do anything wrong. For the officer, the entire situation and the people involved were unknowns. The officer had to utilize *possibility* thinking. Hypervigilance saves cop lives.

The Appeal of the Hypervigilant State

From the beginning of their careers, each time officers put on the uniform and assume the police role, hypervigilance kicks in. A sense of alertness, aliveness, and quick decision making becomes the biological and psychological world of the on-duty police officer. Cops think well on their feet—hypervigilance sees to that. Cops know the feeling of being a cop.

Very few careers create hypervigilance in the work force. Very few careers have workers who begin their careers with such enthusiasm.

For many young officers, the feeling has a recreational sense about it. Many veteran officers who leave police work, for whatever reason, return to the job with the following explanation:

"Cop work gets in your blood."

This subjective state of hyperalertness and elevated thought and emotional responses becomes inseparable from the police role. Very few careers create hypervigilance in the work force. Very few careers have workers who begin their careers with such enthusiasm.

"I love this job. I love being a cop."

New officers say that for the first few years, anyway. Watch young police officers at work and you will see people experiencing hypervigilance. New officers are often experiencing this reaction for the first time in their lives. They just can't get enough of doing the job.

Many people try to experience the hypervigilance of police work vicariously. What other career field has positions, such as many law enforcement agencies have, similar to volunteer or reserve officers? These are men and women who volunteer to attend the police academy, without pay, on their own time. They often incur many expenses for the tools of the trade, such as uniforms, weapons, and equipment, out of their own pockets.

What do reserve officers get for their contribution of time, energy, and commitment? Ask the reserve officer and you might get the more socially acceptable answer of "helping my community" or "trying to make a difference through public service." Get to know the reserve officer a little more personally and you get the real answer. She or he might not use the correct term, but the concept of hypervigilance is in the response:

> *"I get that alive, high-energy, quick-thinking feeling that makes the reds redder and the blues bluer."*

What other career field offers chances for citizens to come out and share the workers' time without being compensated? What other career field has anything like citizen ride-alongs? What do the citizens get for their eight hours in a patrol car with an officer?

> *"I get a front row seat to the greatest show on earth."*

Even on days that are uneventful, when the officer tells the citizen, "Sorry, tonight was kind of slow and you didn't get to see very much," the citizen is thinking, "Are you kidding? I got to see all kinds of stuff." What other career field offers this sense of aliveness, engagement, and quick thinking at work? What other field engages that constant state of elevated alertness, even when nothing is taking place, because the potential for risk always exists? For sure there are other fields that offer hypervigilance. Emergency dispatching, EMS, air traffic control, all offer the hypervigilance experience and all share the downside of the cycle.

On the flip side, what other career field also offers the depression, exhaustion, and desire for social isolation that can typify a law enforcement officer's life at the end of each workday? Hypervigilance is a biologically based action, and every action has an equal and opposite reaction.

Every Action Has an Equal and Opposite Reaction

When an officer goes off duty, the sympathetic branch of the autonomic nervous system, which controls on-duty reactions necessary for survival, gives way to the parasympathetic branch, which controls off-duty reactions. The alert, alive, engaged, quick-thinking individual changes into a detached, withdrawn, tired, and apathetic individual in his or her personal life. Every action has an equal and opposite reaction. *Biological homeostasis*, which is the biological balancing phenomena, turns the person who has been experiencing the hypervigilance reaction based in the sympathetic branch of the autonomic nervous system on duty into the person experiencing the direct opposite parasympathetic reaction off duty.

> *The working officer who socially engages other individuals and practices alert and alive officer safety skills while on duty can have trouble responding to a normal conversation at home.*

Every Action Has an Equal and Opposite Reaction

On Duty

Alive, Alert, Energetic, Involved, Humorous

Normal Range of Risk

Tired, Detached, Isolated, Apathetic

Off Duty

This officer, or "heat seeker," who experiences energy, stimulation, and social interaction and involvement while on duty can turn into the off-duty couch potato. The working officer who socially engages other individuals and practices alert and alive officer safety skills while on duty can have trouble responding to a normal conversation at home. The friend, spouse, or significant other who describes the police officer companion during the off-duty phase of life often makes these observations:

"She is different now that she's a cop."

"He never talks anymore."

"He comes home, sits in front of the TV, and tunes out the world."

"Just sits in front of the computer surfing through nonsense for hours."

"She won't even answer the telephone."

"He just sits on his cellphone playing games."

"When we are out driving, he just looks out the window and says nothing."

The significant other in the officer's life is describing the lower phase of the hypervigilance cycle. "She's different now"—yes, all officers are different. They are experiencing hypervigilance and, in many ways, live in two different biological worlds. One is typified by alertness, involvement, aliveness, and social engagement, while the other world, at home, is typified by exhaustion, isolation, apathy, and on occasion, unfortunately, anger.

On-Duty	Off-Duty
Heat Seeker	**Couch Potato**
(Sympathetic branch)	*(Parasympathetic branch)*
Alert	Tired
Alive	Isolated
Quick thinking	Detached
Good sense of humor	Apathetic
Camaraderie	Angry

What is taking place is a swing between the two aspects of hypervigilance, the on-duty and off-duty phases. Because every action has an equal and opposite reaction, the high demand for more elevated alertness that is required for on-duty police work will produce, unless corrected, an extreme reaction in the opposite direction when off duty. This pendulum-like swing occurs daily in the officer's life. The swings can be conceptualized as a rollercoaster: highs when in the police role (sympathetic autonomic response) followed by lows in the personal role (parasympathetic autonomic response).

Many officers and spouses have not been trained in the Hypervigilance Biological Rollercoaster®, and they find their relationship strained, even broken, by the pendulous swing from alertness at work to indifference at home.

The Hypervigilance
Biological Rollercoaster

What happens to law enforcement officers who move every day between the two different biological worlds of on-duty and off-duty functioning? What are the obstacles officers must overcome to create balanced lives between the two phases of the hypervigilance reaction?

The biological rollercoaster created by hypervigilance can take over the day-to-day lives of police officers and their families and destroy the fabric of their worlds. The capacity to picture or visualize the rollercoaster is essential to understanding the dynamics taking place at work and at home and to learn strategies to break the destructive effect the rollercoaster can produce on police officers and their families.

Hypervigilance keeps officers alive on the street, but they return home to a state that is the opposite of hypervigilance. Without awareness of how the rollercoaster works, an officer's life can become controlled by this pendulous effect. If not mastered, the rollercoaster can become the major force in shaping an officer's life. The downside of the rollercoaster can, without the officer's awareness of its destructive effects, begin determining non-police-related activities and relationships. What is it like for the officer returning home to the downside of the hypervigilance cycle? The upside has a physically pleasant feeling, but the opposite is true of the downside. The following descriptions of officer behavior while off duty tell the story:

“*I know when he's sitting in front of the TV and I'm talking to him, he doesn't hear a word of what I'm saying.***"**

—an officer's wife

"We drove upstate last week to visit my folks. She looked out the window, and all I got were one-word answers. Then all of a sudden, a car sped by us, and she said, 'Why don't I see those assholes when I'm on duty?'"

—an officer's husband

"The only time she says anything at all is when it has something to do with work."

—an officer's son

"He doesn't hardly speak to me, but when someone from work calls on the telephone, he's back alive, full of emotion, questions, and conversation about work. But then when he hangs up the phone and I ask, 'Who was that on the telephone?' all I get is a distant 'Ah, nobody really.'"

—an officer's significant other

"When I come home after work, even though I've been looking forward all day to getting home and seeing my family, I walk through the door and it hits me. I feel drugged. All I want to do is be left alone."

—an officer

"I can sit in front of the TV and surf channels every five seconds and just veg out for hours on end."

—an officer **”**

Case History

Once when I was conducting a training session at a law enforcement agency, a young police spouse approached me on a break and tearfully stated, "Dr. Gilmartin, I'm so worried my marriage is going to fail. We have two small children, and after work all my husband does is sit in front of the computer and play video games. He doesn't talk. I know he loves me and the kids, but he doesn't interact with us. I drag him to parties with my coworkers, and he hates to go. He says they're all a bunch of liberal assholes. He goes into a separate room at the party and just gets on his cellphone. I'm very worried about my marriage."

I asked her if her husband was at the training today. She stated, "No, the chief said it was not mandatory, so he didn't come. He said it was just a bunch of bullshit anyway. I came today because I'm so worried about our marriage."

This two-phase effect of hypervigilance on the life of a law enforcement officer can create challenges to maintaining a balanced personal life. If the challenges are not successfully met or the Hypervigilance Biological Rollercoaster® is not understood, relationships fail, inappropriate behavior increases, and lives can be irreparably broken. Officers who do not understand the up-and-down nature of the rollercoaster only know that they feel more "normal" at work, more "alive" at work. They know that when they walk through the doors to their homes and personal lives, they can feel

This day-to-day cycle of high elevation at work followed by detachment, social isolation, and exhaustion at home redefines the daily pattern for many police officers.

like zombies who don't talk and don't want to do anything—unfortunately, the families suffer greatly and don't know why.

Recovery from the Rollercoaster

Because the hypervigilance rollercoaster is a biological cycle, it will actually self-correct if left alone. For example, after approximately eighteen to twenty-four hours, the effects of hypervigilance will be alleviated, and the person will return to a normal phase of social interaction, emotion, and perception.

The Hypervigilance Recovery Period

On Duty

Alive, Alert, Energetic, Involved, Humorous

Tired, Detached, Isolated, Apathetic

Off Duty

This recovery period raises one very important question, however, for the average police officer:

"What do you typically do within eighteen to twenty-four hours after you return home from work?"

There are several possible responses, such as eat, sleep, or visit with family and friends, but the overriding response in terms of importance and potential impact on the hypervigilance rollercoaster is this:

"Go back to work."

The officer returns to the on-duty world of required safety-based perception, back to the world of hypervigilance. What this creates is a lifestyle based on the swings between the extremes of perceptual alertness caused by the necessity to be hypervigilant (sympathetic branch) on the streets and the opposite reaction of extreme parasympathetic detachment and inactivity at home. This swing becomes the everyday life of the police officer and of the police family.

The Hypervigilance Biological Rollercoaster®

On Duty

Alive, Alert, Energetic, Involved, Humorous

Tired, Detached, Isolated, Apathetic

Off Duty

Two extremes exist every day in the life of a police officer. The problem is, if the officer and family are not aware of the cycle and its potential destruction, they can't be expected to take the appropriate corrective action and avoid the devastating effects on both their personal and professional lives. This day-to-day cycle of high elevation at work followed by detachment, social isolation, and exhaustion at home redefines the daily pattern for many police officers. It also means little time is spent within the normal range or between the lines—*maybe* an officer will hit the normal range while traveling to and from work. The officer, without benefit of training or intervention, now actually exists in two worlds, with what appear to be two lives: the on-duty police life of the sympathetic autonomic response and the off-duty personal life of parasympathetic behavior. Not to be informed of the rollercoaster keeps the officer and family in the dark about what is taking place, what they can do to break this destructive cycle, and how they can do it.

You can't solve a problem if you don't even know what the problem is.

The Magic Chair

In many occupational fields, the workforce returns home exhausted and disengaged from friends and family. Most of these occupational fields, however, see the worker come home exhausted from a long day of physically demanding and sometimes backbreaking labor. The officer also is exhausted—not from having expended extreme amounts of muscular energy, but from the effects of heightened awareness, of hypervigilance. The officer is physically exhausted because the hypervigilance cycle is biological, not psychological. The physiological changes occur first, and they are basis for the psychological and social changes. Many officers unaware of the roll-ercoaster come home and fall into a classic dilemma that haunts many police families: the *magic chair*.

Most police officers, male or female, single or married, have magic chairs. They don't call them by that name, but nonetheless, they possess them and use them almost daily. These are called magic chairs because as soon as officers sit in them, after returning home from work, by "magic" all their blood instantly turns into lead. They can't talk; they can't answer even the most basic question asked by a family member—all they can do is sit and enter into a vegetative off-duty phase. Most frequently, the magic chair is operated in conjunction with an electronic entertainment device for enhanced effect, typically a television set—preferably one with multichannel cable or satellite capacity—a computer, or smart phone.

Here's how it works: The officer approaches the chair, sits in it, and makes some form of ritualistic verbalization, for example, "what a day." This is followed by reaching for the remote control and switching on the television set or going to their favorite social media app. The lower half of the biological rollercoaster is now in operation. All the biological attributes that typified the on-duty, upper reaches of the rollercoaster, such as peripheral vision, acute hearing, rapid thinking, and decision making, are all unnecessary now that survival is no longer at risk—the reverse effects take place. The on-duty attributes are soon replaced by the off-duty attributes until the officer is riding the magic chair to full effect. He or she sees nothing but the computer screen or television set because tunnel vision has taken over. The officer hears nothing but what is being said on the television. Everybody and everything else is blocked out. For how long does the officer watch each channel or read social media? About three to five seconds, on average. This channel changing or scrolling demonstrates that it is not the content of the program or social media posts being viewed that are controlling the focused behavior, just the process of "checking out," detaching from the surrounding environment. This is the direct opposite response from that of the engaged on-duty phase.

The officer is using the magic chair to recover while in the bottom half of the rollercoaster. How long can the average officer remain in the lower phase, switching channels on the television every three to five seconds or aimlessly surfing the internet? Ask officers and many will say something like this:

"Until I fall asleep."

"Eighteen to twenty-four hours, and then I have to go back to work."

Typically, sitting in the magic chair is not in itself a problem. It does not cause any known injury to vital organs or functions. It could, however, be considered a major problem if the officer resides with another life form. This could be a wife, husband, significant other, child, or even a pet cat or dog. The other life form might want to do something "outrageous," like talk. What happens when the other person attempts to transmit a communication to the officer now in the magic chair? It soon becomes clear that the person is transmitting, but the officer is not receiving. The officer has mastered the capacity to tune out. Officers may not know why or how they do it, but they do it very well. When in the magic chair and asked a question by a significant other, the officer doesn't really hear the question but has mastered a unique communication style. She or he has mastered the art of the **nonsense transmission**.

This is a verbal nonresponse to the person who, unfortunately, is attempting to engage the officer in a personal conversation. The nonsense transmission has no inherent content value as a message.

It is a verbal utterance designed solely to keep the person from bothering the off-duty officer who is in magic chair mode.

Nonsense Transmissions
Typical examples of nonsense transmissions:

- "Sure, babe, we'll talk about it later."
- "Whatever you think is fine with me."
- "Why don't you kids go outside and play? I'll look at your homework a little later."
- "Sure, that sounds good."
- "Sure, we'll see."
- "Yeah, maybe."

The nonsense transmission is designed to keep the other person at arm's length and give the appearance of social interaction without being overtly offensive toward the party wishing to interact. The officer hears nothing and sees nothing, which is an effective form of sensory blockage. It is biologically based but can be corrected if officers and significant others know of its existence. If they don't know of its existence, hard feelings, rejection, social isolation, and failed relationships can be the consequences.

The magic chair comes in various modes:

- "I'm watching television" mode
- "I'm on the computer" mode
- "I'm reading the newspaper" mode
- "I'm taking a nap" mode
- "I'm just thinking about something" mode

Magic Chair Test

Anyone in a relationship with a police officer can test for the magic chair phenomena by taking the following steps:

Once you believe the off-duty officer is in the magic chair, engaged in staring at the television set and tuning out the world, begin the test by starting an insignificant conversation while standing approximately six to ten feet to the right or left of the officer. As you transmit statements or questions and receive nonsense transmissions in return, quietly begin moving closer and closer to the officer, until you are standing between the officer and the television set, blocking his or her view of the television.

If the officer says something like, "Come on, honey, step aside; I'm trying to watch this," then the officer doesn't have the condition in an extreme form because he or she is actually acknowledging your presence by interacting with you. If the officer reaches up and gently guides you aside to see the television, the condition is not extreme because he or she is validating your presence by touching you, acknowledging your existence.

If, however, when you quietly step in front of the officer, blocking the view of the television set, and his or her brain goes on autopilot, the unconscious correction mode, and the officer slightly leans to the left or right to look around you without saying a word, the condition exists in an extreme form, and warning bells should go off to address the issue before the relationship suffers harm.

Although it can appear, at first glance, to be a normal, benign form of recovery after a hard day's work, the magic chair phenomenon can start a process of deterioration in the quality of relationships between the police officer and those persons central to his or her personal life. What happens when the lower phase of the rollercoaster becomes the normal way of interacting at home? The relationship stops having the level of emotional energy invested in it that is required to maintain a dynamic, growing relationship. Nothing drastic happens at first; however, gradual erosion is taking place. The family has fewer conversations and spends less time together. When this phenomenon is compounded with the effects of long hours, rotating shift work, and, possibly, moonlighting at an off-duty job, the consequences can begin to destroy even the most solid relationship.

Mistaking the Rollercoaster for Other Problems

Unless officers act to change the lower phase of the cycle, their personal lives will change. If a mental health professional looked at the lower phase of the hypervigilance cycle, noting the isolation, apathy, detachment, and exhaustion, the professional would probably describe the state as depression. Although the lower phase of the Hypervigilance Biological Rollercoaster® produces many aspects similar to depression, it is not true clinical depression. True depression does not involve the rapid thinking processes, social engagement, quick wit, and independent decision making that typifies the on-duty phase of the officer's life. All the mental health professional would need to see is the on-duty phase of the same officer to realize it is not textbook depression that is taking place but rather some type of cyclical change. If this swing of emotional energy could confuse the mental health professional, what about the individual officers and those with whom they share personal lives? Wouldn't they also be confused? Compound the confusion about what is taking place by adding shift work to the equation and many relationships become extremely strained.

Without knowing what is taking place in their lives, they mistakenly conclude that the people and events in their personal lives are causing the change in feelings they are experiencing.

Without insight into what is taking place, not only are significant

Why?

The often-heard "why" questions asked by the significant others in an officer's life show the confusion created by the rollercoaster:

- "Why doesn't he talk anymore when he comes home?"
- "Why don't we do anything anymore?"
- "Why don't we have the 'up' times like we used to have?"
- "Why don't we go anywhere anymore?"
- "Why is everything so negative when she talks?"
- "Why does he just bury himself in social media?"
- "Why when we are in the car does he just stare out the window and not say anything?"
- "Why isn't she ever at home anymore?

others asking questions about what is going on, the officers also are attempting to explain to themselves what they are experiencing. Why do they feel one way at work and another way at home? Some officers, without benefit of information concerning the rollercoaster, come home and experience the downside of the hypervigilance effect and do not understand this emotional elevator drop. They walk through the door and feel tired, disinterested, detached, and, unfortunately, they form incorrect conclusions. Without knowing what is taking place in their lives, they mistakenly conclude that the people and events in their personal lives are causing the change in feelings they are experiencing. They have not been informed that the emotional changes they are experiencing are part of a very predictable biological process that is taking place *inside them* and is not being caused by the people in their lives. Without this knowledge of the impact of hypervigilance, officers can draw incorrect and damaging conclusions that can have devastating long-term effects on their personal lives. The hypervigilance rollercoaster may have visible social and psychological consequences, but the root causes are biological.

It Must Be Their Fault

Without knowing that the emotional and perceptual swing is something taking place biologically within them, officers can mistakenly project responsibility for their emotions onto the home and those in their personal lives:

> *"I guess I love my family, but I really can't stand being there. I walk into the house and realize, man, I don't want to be here. It's not something I can put my finger on. I'm just not happy at home. I get angry at everything, and in my mind, nobody can do anything right. I just want to be left alone. At home they really make me crazy."*

Many officers experience the down cycle repeatedly and they don't know how to solve the issue because they don't know what is taking place. They only know that they feel one way at work and the opposite at home. Work is a fun and challenging place where they feel alive and have lots to do and get involved with; home, on the other hand, is boring.

> *"I'm tired and the last thing I want to do is sit and talk."*

The officers who do not have good emotional survival training in how to break this cycle may practice good street survival skills while at work but then go home and collapse. They experience this cycle each day and cannot identify what is taking place. They have not been informed of the biological flip side of officer safety. They just know the cycle from living it each day.

The Cycle

Go to work, get off duty, go home, get depressed. . . . Go to work, get off duty, go home, get depressed. . . . Go to work, get off duty, go home, get depressed. . . . Go to work, get off duty, go home, get depressed. . . . Go to work, get off duty, go home, get depressed.

How do you break this cycle? Mistakenly, most officers decide:

"Don't go home."

This mistaken conclusion by officers has probably caused more heartache and destruction in police families than all the felons' bullets ever fired.

Don't Go Home

"Don't go home" can become an unconscious way of breaking the cycle. At first, it is not a conscious way of avoiding home as much as a conscious awareness that while on duty, the world is alive, stimulating, and invigorating, and off duty, at home, it is subdued, depressing, and isolating. Staying at work is also consistent with the personal attributes that the law enforcement culture values greatly. Dedication, commitment, and seeing a job through to conclusion are all positive attributes in a contributing professional. They are also easy rationalizations for not going home.

How do officers not go home? Stay at work for long hours. Overtime is very much rewarded in police culture. Unenlightened supervisors and managers can mistakenly confuse this behavior as a high degree of commitment to the police career, which it is in the short run, but clearly this extra work has destructive long-term consequences both personally and professionally. Working overtime shifts is also consistent with the values of providing for loved ones. The dedicated cop has a tough balancing act to perform.

Another way of not going home is stopping after work with fellow officers and having a few drinks, sometimes referred to as the traditional old school "choir practice." It's an attempt to ward off the emotional drop that hits when the officer moves from the on-duty phase of hypervigilance to the off-duty phase. Socializing with fellow officers and families can be an appropriate and healthy activity—if done within reason. This is often a fertile ground, however, for inappropriate and high-risk behaviors that can jeopardize the officer personally and professionally. How many "choir practices" or get togethers have become launching pads for broken relationships and marriages? How many careers and, tragically, lives have ended due to impaired driving and DUI arrests during the officer's journey home?

Another way of not going home can be working off-duty jobs, moonlighting or "detail work." For many officers, off-duty employment has a twofold effect. It clearly assists the family's financial needs but also lets the officer remain in the more alive mode of the officer role. She or he doesn't have to develop other, more constructive strategies or skills for breaking the rollercoaster effect. Although the willingness to do the off-duty or detail work is rooted partly in a well-internalized and commendable work ethic, no matter how noble the cause, "not going home" is the end result.

Disengage

Ask police officers what they enjoy doing after they return home, and many give a simple response:

- "Nothing."
- "Kicking back."
- "Chilling."
- "Relaxing."
- "Vegging out."

What does this disengagement from the nonpolice role of the officer's life look like in terms of the hypervigilance rollercoaster? See the figure below.

The Hypervigilance Biological Rollercoaster®: Disengagement from Personal Life

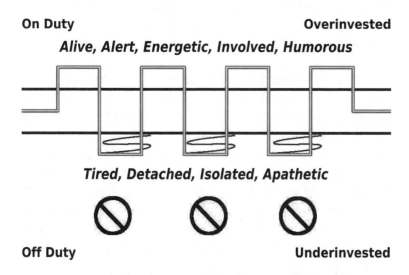

On Duty   **Overinvested**

Alive, Alert, Energetic, Involved, Humorous

Tired, Detached, Isolated, Apathetic

Off Duty   **Underinvested**

Many times the officer basically stops engaging in activities during the lower phase of her or his life. The slashes in the lower phase of the diagram above indicate that off-duty activities can cease to exist as a significant aspect of the officer's life. Officers become significantly *underinvested emotionally* in the personal aspects of their lives. Conversely, they become *overinvested emotionally* in the police role part of their lives.

This investment imbalance, which starts off as naive rookie enthusiasm, can become a damaging situation of *The lower phase, or off-duty life, of the officer tragically becomes of secondary importance.* being emotionally overinvested in the police role and can create destruction along multiple dimensions of officers' lives. The obvious first dimension to be affected is in an officer's personal life. All aspects of the officer's personal life can become associated with, or "tainted" by, the lower phase of the cycle. Everything to do with work is associated with the upper phase. The lower phase, or off-duty life, of the officer tragically becomes of secondary importance.

Unfortunately, so do many of the people who play emotional roles in the personal life of the officer. This disengagement can obviously be very destructive in dyadic adult relationships, but how much more destructive is it for the parenting role, especially single parents bearing the sole responsibility of raising their children?

Symptoms of the Hypervigilance Rollercoaster

How does an officer know if she or he is falling victim to the hypervigilance cycle and its effects of home avoidance and work overinvestment?

If an officer or significant other is trying to determine the effect of the rollercoaster on their relationship, each should know the symptoms. Following are the first warning signs, or symptoms, that an officer is falling victim to the hypervigilance rollercoaster. (See chapter 8 for corrective strategies and ways to address the lower phases of the rollercoaster and maintain a balanced emotional perspective.)

1. **The desire for social isolation at home:** Officers can find themselves being noncommunicative, withdrawn, and apathetic concerning family activities. Officers assume their domestic partner will take care of "all the mundane activities" such as raising kids, paying the bills, maintaining the home, and having a personal life. This is demonstrated by the officer riding the magic chair of internet surfing or TV watching after spending an on-duty day as a heat seeker.

2. **Unwillingness to engage in conversation or activities that are not police related:** This effect is obvious to any observer at a police social encounter. Go to the party and notice how the conversation revolves around "war stories." One of the reasons for this type of social interaction is that as each verbal exchange takes place, and each story is told, the officers listening to the war story vicariously experience the physiological reaction of returning to hypervigilance. Telling war stories and socializing with other officers gets the blood flowing. It has tremendous antidepressant effects. It moves the people, both those telling the war stories and those

listening, back up to the upper phase of the rollercoaster by producing short-term physical stimulation. It really feels good to tell war stories in the earlier years of a law enforcement career. The socialization process by which officers interact, taking turns telling war stories, can be called *adrenal masturbation*—it has exciting short-term physical consequences but is totally nonproductive. Unfortunately, this form of social interaction doesn't just occur during the early years of a law enforcement career and potentially stifles the social interaction of many veteran law enforcement officers. This can be seen with veteran police officers who begin feeling comfortable only socializing with other cop types who have shared their socialization experiences. Many times veteran officers enter the post-police work retirement years very vulnerable emotionally and socially.

3. **Reduced interaction with nonpolice friends and acquaintances:** Officers spend their time with other officers. Squad parties, choir practices, and other social encounters revolving around work become the socialization pattern to the exclusion of old friends. Often officers will rationalize the closed social network of primarily socializing with other officers: "I get tired of these other people. Once they find out you're a cop, all they want to do is complain about some ticket they got or something. I don't want to talk about work." Actually, this particular rationalization, or excuse, is the direct opposite of reality. One of the reasons cops, particularly young cops, don't like to talk or socialize with friends who are not in police work is "those other folks don't have any good stories." They live pretty mundane, boring lives. The nonpolice friends live "between the lines." They don't have any great war stories to tell. Picture an interaction between an officer of two or three years in law enforcement and an old nonpolice friend who sells fencing material.

The friend relates, "John, I just sold 8,500 feet of chain link fence to the school district."

The officer thinks, *So what? Who gives a damn?*

Only the feeling of being on the upper level of the hyper-vigilance rollercoaster, either at work or while socializing, validates a feeling of aliveness or self-worth for the officer. Everything else is boring.

4. **Procrastination in decision making not related to work:** Officers can begin withdrawing from decision making and any self-initiated off-duty activities. An example of this is in the following case history.

Case History

This example concerns a highly active police officer who has no trouble making complex decisions during the workday. He routinely makes complex decisions concerning tactical issues and search-and-seizure questions. In addition to his full-time assignment, he also functions as an operations supervisor for his agency's SWAT team.

One day, while en route home from work, the officer receives a text message from his spouse, asking him to stop and pick up some groceries. The officer enters the store approximately twenty minutes after getting off duty and he walks right past me (a coworker of many years) and does not recognize me. After shopping, the officer gets in the line to check out his groceries, giving an external impression of "doing the zombie shop." He puts the groceries on the conveyor belt, and the clerk scans the groceries and engages the officer in the following conversation:

Clerk: Good evening, sir.
Officer: [inaudible grunt]

Clerk: How are you tonight, sir?
Officer: [second inaudible grunt]

Clerk: What will that be for tonight, sir, paper or plastic?
Officer: [third inaudible grunt]

Clerk: What will that be for tonight, sir, paper or plastic?
Officer: [heavy sigh, hesitation] Surprise me.

Obviously, "surprise me" isn't an answer; it's an abdication of an answer. It is an abandonment of any responsibility to make a decision. The officer is probably rationalizing his nonanswer with some thoughts

> *Withdrawal from decision making can leave the officer's significant other with a sense of abandonment and, on occasion, a feeling of being overwhelmed by the responsibility of running the household on his or her own.*

along the lines of "who gives a shit?" (a common police rationalization for noninvolvement in decision making and nonparticipation in non-police-related activities)—it was just a grocery bag. If this type of nonparticipation or procrastination in decision making were used only in situations of the magnitude of "paper or plastic," it would not pose a difficulty in the officer's personal life. Unfortunately, however, even in major decisions that police families are required to make on a day-to-day basis, the officer member is often not present, participating, or involved. As one police spouse answered a question I posed:

Author: How many children do you have?
Police spouse: Counting my husband?

Author: Counting your husband, what do you mean?
Police spouse: Well, he's like another child. I mean, if we're going on a trip or something, I have to pack for the kids, and then I have to pack for him. Otherwise he doesn't bring anything and complains because he doesn't have any clothes or anything. It's easier just to count him as one of the kids.

It might be easier in the short run "to count him as one of the kids," but what impact on the relationship does this abdication of responsibility have on any sense of adult partnership?

"I've been making decisions all week. Whatever you want is fine with me."

This statement, along with the paper or plastic dilemma, illustrates how many officers can make wonderful decisions while functioning in the upper phase of the hypervigilance rollercoaster, but cannot or do not want to make even the most basic decisions while in the lower phases.

This withdrawal from decision making can leave the officer's significant other with a sense of abandonment and, on occasion, a feeling of being overwhelmed by the responsibility of running the household on his or her own. One spouse told of her officer-husband who heard on the evening news that mortgage rates were falling and announced to his spouse: "Honey, why don't you take care of refinancing the house and see what kind of a new mortgage rate we can get." The idea of making a joint decision on the mortgage was not even spoken of—only the concept "you handle it; I got stuff at work to do." This withdrawal from involvement in one's own personal life has major implications in the overall functioning in both the officer's personal and professional realms.

5. **Infidelity:** This is one of the most painful aspects of the hypervigilance rollercoaster. Anything associated with "home" or the lower phase of the rollercoaster is boring, and anything associated with the upper phase is exciting, stimulating, and dynamic. Without insight or training in the effects of the rollercoaster, relationships shatter. People meeting and interacting during the upper phases appear brighter, wittier, prettier, more handsome—"the reds are redder, and the blues are bluer." Emotions surge and individuals, particularly those experiencing the strain caused by the rollercoaster in their personal lives, find a terribly destructive way not to go home—they go to someone else's home.

Infidelity begins with the surging emotions shared at the upper phase of the rollercoaster. People bond when they share risk. This has always accounted for the close relationships among police officers. It has become more complex, as has the overall workplace, with both genders represented in more equal proportions in recent years. The failure of some clearly dysfunctional marriages and relationships are readily understandable to an outside observer who knew the relationship; however, some relationship failures defy a strictly logical explanation when one sees the new individual with whom the officer has become involved. Case histories point out the painful consequences and total bewilderment that can be experienced by the partner left behind by new relationships that, many times, are superficially initiated and based only on time shared in the upper phase of the rollercoaster.

These relationships tend to be rapidly forming, intense, and often typified by abrupt changes in the behavior of the officer, such as abandoning her or his marriage or existing relationship. The new relationship, many times, has elements that resemble an adolescent's running away from home. Officers leaving the previously existing relationship often feel extreme guilt; however, they simultaneously feel a tremendous sense of freedom and aliveness to be out of the existing relationship or marriage. They may have tragically formed the wrong conclusion and believed the existing marriage or relationship itself was the source of their unfulfilled feelings and depression. The reality, in many cases, is that it was the effects of the hypervigilance rollercoaster taking a destructive toll on the law enforcement officer and the people in his or her personal life.

Case History

I don't know why she is doing this. I think I have been very supportive of her. I did all the work here at home while she went to the police academy. I took care of the kids and did all the housework, in addition to my own job, which is never just forty hours a week. Is it something I did? What can I do to win her back?

I try to understand and be supportive of her police work. I think I really am. I wasn't wild about her going into the police department, but it was something she wanted to do. She's my life partner, so I supported her decision. I helped her in the academy with her notebooks and typing.

(continued)

I know it was really hard physically for her, and she was always tired, so I made sure I helped. I retyped her class notes each day. I shined her leather for inspections—heck, I was in the Marines, and I actually spit-shined her boots and leather every night after she went to sleep, so she could get eight hours of rest. I would do anything to get her back. I think she's totally forgotten about me and the kids. She started running around with one of the cops she works with, and, and, hell, he's married, and I guess it's breaking up that marriage, too. I don't know what changed her thinking. We've been together for twelve years, and I thought something like this would never happen to us.

Case History

I don't know why he wants to end the marriage. I know I have gained some weight since we got married, but not that much. I've had two babies. I try to look pretty for him. If he's interested in being physical, I try to never turn him away, even when he comes home at those oddball hours in the middle of the night. I don't know what he sees in her. She's a waitress at the café all the cops hang out at. I know she's been going to the squad parties; one of the other wives told me. I can't see him giving up his family, the kids, the house, and the marriage for her. I mean, she's nothing to look at, and I hear her kids are already in trouble with the law. Her ex-husband has been in prison. I don't understand what has gotten into him. He has always been so level headed. I can't explain how our whole world fell apart so fast.

6. **Noninvolvement in children's needs and activities:** In many law enforcement families, children interact with the officer parent only in the lower reaches of the rollercoaster. Several case histories can demonstrate this.

Case History

A forty-two-year-old narcotics sergeant calls me from a jurisdiction approximately 150 miles away and asks if he can have an appointment to discuss a criminal profiling question. I inquire if the information can be discussed on the telephone, saving the sergeant an approximately three-hour drive to my office. The sergeant is more than willing to drive the three hours and relates that he would feel more comfortable discussing the case in person. So we make the appointment, and the sergeant arrives for his scheduled meeting.

After approximately twenty-five minutes of discussing the criminal profiling question, the sergeant stands, prepares to leave my office, and states, "Well, I guess that means it's over?" I assume the sergeant means the appointment to discuss the criminal profiling case and reply, "No, if you think we need more time, I have the next two hours open," whereupon the sergeant begins crying and says, "No, I mean, I guess that means his childhood is over." I am caught totally unprepared for the sergeant's statement and the emotional reaction that seems totally outside the context of the criminal profiling discussion.

I ask, "What's going on?" The sergeant tearfully relates, "I guess that means his childhood is over. I always thought I was going to be the kind of father that did things with his kids, you know, went camping and hiking and took them to baseball games. Well, it really hit me hard about two weeks ago. My youngest son, who is eighteen, just went into the Marine Corps. He left for bootcamp, and it really hit me hard. I have three kids, and I never did any of those things with them. I always thought I would, but there was always another dope deal to work or another search warrant to do. I have been breaking down crying since he left at the airport.

(continued)

My wife says, 'Honey, it will be okay, it's just his time to go and do the things in life he wants to do. It will be okay.' I can't figure it out. She's doing okay, and I'm breaking down crying now for two weeks. It's not that I just miss my boy. It's that I realize I missed his childhood. I think my wife is doing better with this than me because she did all those things with him. She was the Cub Scout mom, the soccer mom, hell, she was always doing stuff with all three of the kids and worked full time besides. I never did shit with the kids. I love them, but I guess you have to show it with your actions, not with just what you feel inside. You have to put those feelings into action. I wish I could do it all over again!"

Case History

I am instructing a class at a large police department in an eastern state when a young police officer approaches me during a class break, immediately after a discussion of the hypervigilance rollercoaster. The young officer inquires, "Do you know how long I've known my father for?" I, not ever having met the officer before, am somewhat bewildered by the question and respond that I have no idea how long the officer has known his father.

The young officer responds, "Of course not," and continues, "I've known my father for five years—oh, don't get me wrong, I was raised in a home with my father present, but I never knew him. I met my father five years ago when I became a police officer. My father is a lieutenant in this department, and when I arrived at the academy and people saw my last name on my name tag, all I heard was 'You must be Lt. _____'s son. Your dad is a hell of a guy.'

"I would hear about my dad from everybody I met. They would tell me about my dad and what they had done together. One cop tells me, 'I'll never forget your dad. The day my wife was in a terrible car accident, I was working on his squad. He spent the whole night and most of the next day with me waiting at the hospital until my wife was out of the woods. Your dad is one hell of a great guy. I'd do anything for him.'

"It wasn't until right now, hearing you talk about that hypervigilance rollercoaster, that I realized all those cops knew the man at the top half of the rollercoaster; growing up, I only knew the man at the bottom half of the rollercoaster. Since I became an officer, I see my father almost every day. Now we have a great relationship. We talk all the time, mostly about the department and everything, but then we talk about all kinds of other stuff. He comes over to my house and helps me with projects at my place and does stuff with my kids. I find myself over helping Mom and him on stuff around their house. Growing up, it wasn't that he did anything bad at home. He just never did anything. Cops should be taught about this rollercoaster so they can do what they have to do to make it right at home. I'm lucky I became a cop and got to know my father. My brothers are not cops, and they probably don't see our father three times a year. All my brothers know is the man at the bottom of the rollercoaster. What a loss for police families when they don't learn this stuff until it is too late!"

7. **The "I usta" syndrome—loss of interest in hobbies or recreational activities:** To see the effects of the hypervigilance rollercoaster on off-duty activities, ask an officer to describe his or her personal life. When I inquire specifically about what officers like to do when they are not doing police work, I often receive an interesting set of responses:

Question:	Tell me a little about yourself.
Officer's answer:	I work uniform patrol in the second shift. Been there about five years.
Question:	Do you like it?
Officer's answer:	Yeah, it's okay. You know the normal stuff, lots of calls. Yeah, I like it. I like being a cop here with this department.
Question:	What about your personal life?
Officer's answer:	Well, I'm married. My spouse works over at the hospital. We have two kids.
Question:	That's great. What do you like to do when you're not working, you know, hobbies or non-work-related activities?
Officer's answer:	I really like to go fishing. I am really into that. We got some great streams and lakes not far from here at all.
Question:	That's great! How often do you get out fishing?
Officer's answer:	I try to get out as often as I can.
Question:	That's great, but when was the last time you went fishing?
Officer's answer:	Oh, I don't know, it has been a while. Like I said, I like to get out as often as I can.
Question:	But when exactly was the last time you went fishing?
Officer's answer:	Exactly, boy, I don't know. You know we're real short in the field right now, and we're waiting for that academy class to graduate to put a few more people on the street.
Question:	Okay, but exactly when was the last time you went fishing?
Officer's answer:	Exactly? Oh, I don't know exactly, but like I said, we're real short of officers in the field. Exactly, I guess, I don't know maybe, exactly. To tell you the truth, I guess it's been about two years, but *I usta* go all the time.

"I Usta"

- "I usta fish."
- "I usta do crafts and handiwork."
- "I usta hunt."
- "I usta jog."
- "I usta take my kids to the park."
- "I usta sew."
- "I usta work out."
- "I usta read to my kids."
- "I usta go to church."
- "I usta go camping."
- "I usta visit my folks."

- "I usta see old friends."
- "I usta lift weights."
- "I usta keep my house picked up and tidy."
- "I usta sing in the church choir."
- "I usta lay out my uniform the night before so it looked sharp, and I'd shine my leather."
- "I usta do woodworking."
- "I usta garden."

How many of the above sound familiar to you?

The "I usta" phase can deteriorate even further into more generalized senses of loss:

"I usta to be married."

"I usta to have a personal life."

"I usta to give a damn about this job."

The "I usta" response is given by many law enforcement officers to describe any inquiry into their personal lives. It describes what they "**usta**" do before becoming police officers. The "I usta" syndrome is basically a statement that all those activities that existed before becoming a police officer, that helped define the officer as a complete person, have been put on the back burner. They are the activities that get lost because they occur at the bottom half of the rollercoaster.

The "I usta" syndrome is basically a statement that all those activities that existed before becoming a police officer, that helped define the officer as a complete person, have been put on the back burner.

The "I usta" syndrome is a description of the things that have been lost from the officer's life, the things that are not work related and that reside at the bottom of the rollercoaster. This is a lost part of life, the nonpolice personal life, the part where all the other nonwork, nonpolice aspects of life are experienced, such as family, hobbies, and interests. This is also the part of the police officer's life that provides the complete picture of the whole person. It is the phase that keeps officers' lives together and balanced through the trying times and tragic experiences that occur in every police career.

The "I usta" syndrome is the generalized effect of the hypervigilance rollercoaster on the personal interests and nonpolice behaviors of the officer. All the activities that defined the complete man or woman before he or she became a police officer can be lost. If these other parts of life are lost, a new person emerges, many times a new person without the balancing strengths of multiple dimensions, activities, or roles in life to draw on for perspective and understanding. Without this balance, the short-term day-to-day effects of the hypervigilance rollercoaster begin to turn into long-term, more damaging losses.

8. **Incremental weight gain:** As the years progress across a law enforcement career, and the off-duty personal life of the officer constricts as a result of the "I usta" syndrome, the waist size of the officer expands proportionately. This is due not only to the reduction of activity and lack of exercise off duty, but also, physiologically, to the long-term effects of living a life balancing the spiking blood glucose brought on by the hypervigilance cycle and the pancreatic insulin

secretions infusing fats cells with glucose. Unaddressed, this cycle potentially leads to insulin resistance and type 2 diabetes, with elevated risks of heart disease and stroke. (More on this in chapter 8.)

9. **Sleep disorder:** Ironically, the feeling of detachment and exhaustion after the police workday does not lead to a healthy daily sleep pattern. Excessive exposure to video or television screens, shift work, and irregular work-sleep schedules profoundly impact sleep hygiene. Seven to eight hours of quality sleep are required to maintain wellness. Judgment and reaction time in police officers can be impaired by sleep deficiencies by as much as 600 percent compared to factory workers performing shift work. Twenty-four hours of sustained wakefulness yields judgment and reaction times equivalent to having .10 blood alcohol level (BAL). Eighteen hours of sustained wakefulness makes judgment and reaction times the equivalent of .08 BAL. Judgment and reaction times are core to officer safety. In one research project, 83 percent of police officers reported inadequate sleep. Hypervigilance turns the brain on to a heightened mode of alertness for officer safety. Learning healthy ways to turn it down are absolutely required.

Long-Term Effects of Hypervigilance

Police training is designed to prepare officers to work the streets, to handle calls safely, and to practice good officer safety and street survival skills. That would be enough if officers were being asked to work the streets for only a few short years. A comparison of law enforcement with the military might help clarify the effects of long-term versus short-term exposure to a culture of risk.

Military versus Law Enforcement

The military also prepares people for total immersion into a culture of potential risk, although most military personnel will spend an enlistment duration of four or so years on active duty and then leave the military for a return to civilian life. The military knows that it is a relatively short-term role for the individual to assume. *Most police agencies train new officers to be sprinters, and then they enter them into a marathon.*

Clearly during war time, the military has the burden of addressing trauma exposure with its personnel before they leave active service. The military has an expectation, however, of shortened time commitment to the role. Law enforcement organizations train their personnel for total immersion into their own unique culture of potential risk, but unlike the military, every four or so years, the vast majority of police officers do not leave. Most law enforcement officers see their occupational choice of law enforcement as a long-term professional career commitment, not something they move out of after four years. Many officers would say, "You are just learning to be an effective cop after four years."

The training priorities and orientation of many law enforcement agencies produce enthusiastic rookies and, later, bitter and angry veterans. This process can be explained with an analogy: Most police agencies train new officers to be sprinters, and then they enter them into a marathon. The police career choice for many officers is a twenty-year or longer commitment. New officers start out highly enthusiastic, not able to get enough of police work; then, as the years go by, many officers go through some rather drastic changes in terms of how they view police work.

"I love this job."

changes to

"I hate this job and can't wait until I'm out of here."

Which Officers Are Most at Risk?

Who is most prone to experience the effects of the hypervigilance rollercoaster, the best law enforcement officers or the worst? Clearly the answer is the best officers, the most dedicated, the most committed, the most highly motivated—the ones practicing the best hypervigilance and officer safety. These are the men and women who are dedicated to being the best possible officers they can be. Often, they begin their career with only naive enthusiasm as a survival tactic for the emotional dimension of their lives. They are trained in how to handle the streets. They just aren't trained in how to handle the job and its effects on their personal lives. Law enforcement training has made progress in the past decade on processing the reactions to significant traumatic events but appears to still not address the biological and psychological consequences good officers experience while practicing everyday officer safety.

If our best personnel are at highest risk of this phenomenon, who pays the price first? Who is the first victim of the hypervigilance rollercoaster? When I asked this question of a group of officers, one responded:

"That curve describes my life. You must be looking in my window—that's how I live. I have been a cop for eight years now, and I really love it. I work in a part of town that really goes all the time. We run from call to call, but I really love it. I could transfer to a slower division, but I like working down here in this division, where there is lots of activity, but when I get off duty and go home, just like you say, I go through a mind melt. I want to be left alone. I sit in front of the TV. I don't say anything. I don't even answer the telephone if it rings. I let voice mail get it. Your rollercoaster is exactly right in describing me."

At this point, I reiterated my question: "Thank you for your feedback on my concept of the hypervigilance model; however, the question that I asked was 'Who was the first victim?'"

The officer, after some reflection and thought, responded: "Well, the first victim, well, it's the first wife."

The female officers in the class concurred: "The first husband."

Then one female officer responded by saying, "It is not the first husband or the first wife. If you're married, it will affect your marriage, but this curve affects me and I'm not married, I've never been married, and, judging by the men I see at work each day, I assure you I'll never choose to get married. The first victim of this rollercoaster is you and your personal life."

Who Is the First Victim?

The officer is actually the first victim of the rollercoaster dynamic, although clearly many other people are affected by the loss of emotional and behavioral balance in an officer's life. As the number of non-police-related dimensions in officers' lives shrinks, officers are redefined. As the nonpolice aspects of officers' lives (or the things that they "usta" do) diminish, well-balanced individuals can be transformed into people who obtain most of their social and emotional needs from the police role. Everything else is put on the back burner or lost due to the "I usta" syndrome, which is brought on by the hypervigilance rollercoaster.

The nonpolice dimensions of officers' lives, such as spirituality, cultural and ethnic identification, core values, family, friends, hobbies, and other perceptual sets, or ways of viewing the world, reduce if not disappear. The men and women who began their police career as bright, well-rounded, ethical officers begin experiencing major behavioral deficits in their personal lives. Because of the "I usta" syndrome, officers can begin distancing themselves from core aspects of their sense of self. The officer's identity becomes tied only to the police role.

Many people begin police work emotionally and socially well-balanced. The highly selective employment requirements ideally screen out the emotionally and socially deficient from beginning a police career. The lower phase of the rollercoaster, however, causes officers to stop engaging in activities that are not police related when they're off duty. Some officers will reject this concept and say, "I went fishing last week," but if you probe further, you discover that, yes, the officer did go fishing last week, but he or she went with the squad. The question would need to be asked: Was it really a fishing trip? Or a choir practice with fishing rods? What was the main point of the trip? To relax and enjoy some activities with family and friends, or to spend time yet again in an ever-tightening social group? A group that can unfortunately limit its interests solely to the happenings of police work and its individual police agency.

Officers who previously defined themselves by multiple aspects of their lives now define themselves by the singular dimension of their police role.

The degree of emotional and social balance of individuals entering law enforcement before the "I usta" syndrome takes place is graphically demonstrated below:

Before the "I Usta" Syndrome

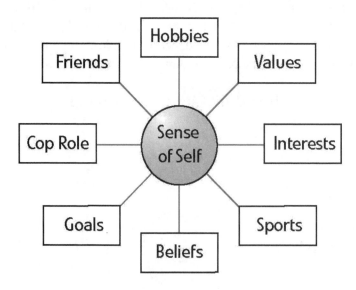

Those entering law enforcement have multiple dimensions in their lives, which add to their overall definition of themselves as complete people. They invest time and energy into numerous aspects of their lives, such as

- spirituality
- culture or ethnicity
- hobbies and interests
- friends
- family
- goals
- physical fitness

Obviously, this list is not exhaustive. Each person has unique attributes that individually define her or him as a person. The emotional anchoring of multiple dimensions and support systems in a person's life determines his or her individual emotional resiliency, stability, and capacity to maintain perspective. As the young officer is exposed to the need to practice hypervigilance to survive the risks of the street, the rollercoaster takes effect, and the nonpolice attributes, support systems, and other life dimensions shrink. The "I usta" syndrome can change the previous graphic into the one below:

After the "I Usta" Syndrome

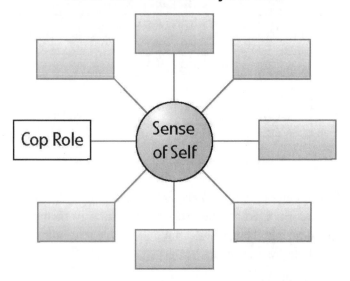

All other supporting dimensions or interests in the officer's life have basically disappeared. Officers who previously defined themselves by multiple aspects of their lives now define themselves by the singular dimension of their police role. They might still pay lip service to the other dimensions of their lives, the things they "usta" do, but the rollercoaster has created behavioral deficits in the number of areas or dimensions in which the officers are investing emotional energy and time.

The sense of self is the total of all the separate dimensions of the individual that combine to define him or her as a unique, free-thinking, independent, and responsible person. The hypervigilance rollercoaster and the "I usta" syndrome clearly can have an impact on the sense of self of the individual who entered law enforcement and may cause significant emotional transformation during the journey from "the person" to "the officer." As behavioral activities of the off-duty phase of the rollercoaster continue to diminish, the sense of self continues to constrict. The broad-based sense of self at the time of entry into the field reduces to identification with only the police role. Officers who have experienced this redefinition of their sense of self do not say:

"I work as a cop."

They say:

"I am a cop."

I Am a Cop

This can be an expression of significant and justifiable pride in being a law enforcement officer, or it can be an indication of significant *overidentification* with the police role and potentially a problematic perspective for the officer.

"I am a cop" defines the essential core of the sense of self for the officer.

"I am a cop" can transform a positive sense of pride in the professional role into an overshadowing of the other essential aspects of the officer's life and identity (or sense of self). It can create a significant *underidentification* with other life roles that balance each other and the cop role.

The loss of nonpolice dimensions in officers' lives due to the lower phase of the rollercoaster can, in one sweep of the brush, cause them to begin having emotional and personal difficulties at the beginning of their career. Progressing across the span of a law enforcement career, this reduction of the sense of self can produce an emotionally fragile individual. This error in the emotional investment portfolio can cause significant harm to the once idealistic officer. The officer's identity has been reduced from the previously broad-based sense of self to a sense of self with only one dimension:

"I am a cop."

Roles that Can Balance the Cop Role
The following are examples of roles that an officer can underidentify with as a result of overidentifying with the cop role.

"I am a friend."

"I am a mother/father."

"I am a husband/wife."

"I am a church/synagogue member."

"I am a bowler."

"I am a hunter."

"I am an embroiderer."

"I am a gardener."

"I am a golfer."

"I am a mountain biker."

The effects of this overidentification emotionally with the police role and the reducing of the sense of self to one dimension have significant impact on the personal and work relationships of the officer in numerous ways. As the officer's sense of self becomes increasingly one-dimensional, the officer becomes more at risk emotionally.

Who's in Control?

What would appear as an intense sense of pride in the profession of police work actually makes the officer significantly more fragile emotionally for a few reasons: One reason is that the "I usta" syndrome has reduced the number of available emotional support systems for the officer to rely on, if needed. A second reason stems from a basic concept of human autonomy:

Who controls the type of person you are?

Functional and healthy human beings maintain some control over their sense of self. They believe they have a degree of autonomy over their existence and have a major say in the events affecting their lives. People need to believe they have a significant degree of control over their own day-to-day existence, a sense of predictability to most major events affecting their lives. This sense of control is a core element in creating a sense of emotional equilibrium or stability. The greater the degree of control or autonomy an individual has in her or his life, the greater the degree of empowerment, stability, and autonomy she or he will experience emotionally. Stress or psychological dysfunction itself, many times, can be defined as the presence of low control in a person's life. Any situation that reduces the individual's degree of control in his or her own life can precipitate a sense of psychological distress. If the loss of control is combined with high demands the individual must handle, the degree of psychological imbalance or stress can be extremely high.

> *People need to believe they have a significant degree of control over their own day-to-day existence, a sense of predictability to most major events affecting their lives.*

Psychological dysfunction has two components:

High Demands

+

Low Control

As predictability, autonomy, and control of the sense of self decrease in a person's life, a sense of emotional vulnerability, susceptibility, and risk increase. As police officers decrease the number of dimensions or roles defining their sense of self and become increasingly invested in only the police role, they increase their level of emotional vulnerability.

A Sense of Singular Identity

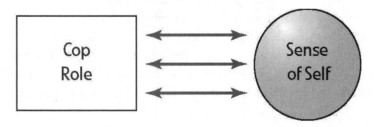

The officer's sense of self is defined by the singular role of being an officer. The sense of self and the job role have become welded together and are basically inseparable: "I *am* a cop." If having a sense of autonomy and a degree of control over the events affecting one's life is essential for an emotionally healthy individual, how does the overidentification with the police role affect the officer? The easiest way to explain how overidentification with the police role can destroy an emotionally healthy individual is to demonstrate the concept of the need to have autonomy or control in one's life. As an officer's sense of self becomes increasingly linked to the police role, who controls his or her police role? Ask officers this question:

"Who decides what kind of cop you're going to be?"

I've asked this question of large numbers of police officers for many years, and their answer is always the same:

"I do. I decide what kind of cop I am going to be."

At first glance, this response may appear to be an expression of emotional autonomy or self-responsibility. It would appear to be a sign of emotionally healthy, responsible individuals who see themselves in charge of their own behavior and who are willing to take responsibility for their own actions. The question and its response, however, are double-edged swords. The following exchange with a homicide detective demonstrates the potential dilemma.

Detective: I decide what kind of cop I am going to be; it is up to me. I'm a homicide detective. I am very good at being a homicide detective. I've worked homicide for over eight years. I've testified in well over one hundred homicide cases. I'm an expert in several aspects of homicide investigation. I've attended many specialized schools on death investigation. I get a significant sense of satisfaction out of working as a homicide detective. I take pride in my job, and it is up to me to control my role and decide what kind of a homicide detective I am going to be.

Initially, the homicide detective's response appears to demonstrate an individual who is willing to take responsibility for his own behavior, a core element of emotionally stable individuals. The potential emotional vulnerability and at-risk situation of this detective can be demonstrated by asking a few straightforward questions.

Author: Sounds like you're a real competent homicide detective and take a great deal of pride in the job you do. It is a very necessary job, and I'm sure you get a sense of purpose, pride, and accomplishment from the job. Let me ask you, though, could you be approached right now by some boss from your agency, some high-ranking person, a chief, a commander, or someone higher on the food chain than you, could they walk up to you and tap you on the shoulder and make you a non-homicide detective? Could they transfer you to a different investigations section or, even worse, back to uniform patrol?

Detective: Yeah, the boss could do all that to me in a New York minute.

Author: I'm confused. You just told me you decide what kind of homicide detective you are going to be. Now you say that the boss is the one who decides. Which is it? Do you decide or does the boss decide your role as a homicide detective?

This interchange demonstrates the clear emotional vulnerability of the competent, dedicated police officer who has become emotionally vulnerable by having a one-dimensional sense of self, of overidentifying with the cop role, a role that consists of several dimensions that the officer clearly does not control.

Officers do not control many of the core issues of their jobs. They do not control many of the central aspects of the cop role. If the cop role and the sense of self have become identical, then the officer does not control her or his sense of self. This creates a significant sense of emotional vulnerability for the police officer:

If the job becomes your life, and you don't control your job, then you don't control your life.

What *Do* Officers Control?

There clearly are dimensions of the police role that law enforcement officers have absolute autonomy and control over. Officers clearly control

- their integrity
- their professionalism
- how well they do the job assigned

However, forces outside the officers themselves control almost everything else concerning the police role. These other forces control major elements of the individuals cop role:

- the agency
- administration or management
- the courts
- the constitution
- the politics of the department
- local, state, or federal elected officials
- the media

Officers control 100 percent of their integrity and professionalism. Everything else—policies, uniforms, required procedures, budget, assignments, organizational goals, and just about every other central aspect of the officer's role—is controlled by someone else.

> Officers control 100 percent of their integrity and professionalism.

Singular Identity Controlled by Others

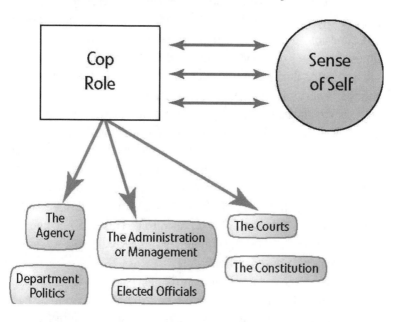

Injustices

Many police officers have firsthand experience of the dynamic of having control taken away from them by forces further up the administrative food chain. How many good cops have overidentified with their jobs and had the rude awakening of

- being taken out of detectives
- getting pulled off the SWAT team
- being transferred back to uniformed patrol

- being transferred to midnight shift
- being transferred out of K-9 and having the dog taken away
- losing a good case to another detective or agent
- having the worst car in the fleet
- being unfairly labeled a racist by the media for just doing their job

It is the rare officer who has not experienced this phenomenon at some point in his or her police career. In the vernacular of the average cop, this is called *getting screwed*. Sometimes the transfers are done for some rational reason that makes sense, and sometimes they are "total bullshit" and reflect some manager, boss, or administrator flexing muscle only to demonstrate that he or she has the capacity to make your life miserable.

Officers unaware of the dynamic of emotional overidentification taking place in their lives can find themselves going through significant emotional turmoil. A sense of vulnerability leads to emotional susceptibility, which is a feeling of being constantly at emotional risk. The officer who has difficulty with overidentification with the police role runs the risk of feeling constantly in emotional danger from the forces that control the police role. This can become an ever-present sense of feeling emotionally at risk, vulnerable, susceptible, threatened, and paranoid.

As some force outside their control affects the cop role, officers who overidentify with the police role find the impact on their personal lives not far behind. The sense of self also takes a hit.

Here, for example, is our homicide detective when he is called into the boss's office and told he is being taken off a major homicide investigation, even though he knows he is the best detective for the case. Worse yet, he is told to go get his uniforms ready because he is being transferred out of detectives and back to patrol. The figure "Singular Identity Controlled by Others" demonstrates the sense of risk the officer experiences every time some force outside his or her control affects the cop role. It is at this point that our homicide detective and probably most other well-intentioned officers who have not

Emotional Effects of a Singular Identity

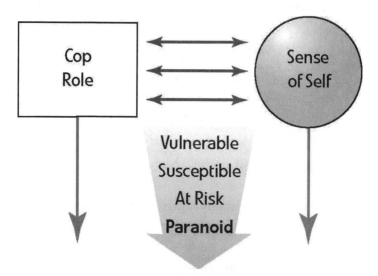

practiced good emotional survival skills begin feeling overwhelming senses of distrust, anger, and open hostility toward the management hierarchy of their own agencies. It is at this point that the police officers who have been unknowingly experiencing the hypervigilance rollercoaster become engaged in the psychological conflict that stems from overidentification with a role they do not control.

The Blame Game

After listening to officers, an observer might encounter the typical phenomenon that engulfs many well-intentioned but poorly informed cops. The locations of the agencies might be quite different, but the officers' responses are almost always identical:

"I can handle the assholes on the street. The assholes that I can't handle are the ones running this place."

"I can do the job if the assholes in the administration would just let us do the damn job. Hell, they don't want us doing the job. The surest way to get in

trouble at this agency is to go out on the streets and do police work. The bosses will screw you to the wall if you do good cop work. They want us out there making kumbaya with all the assholes."

"Oh yeah, right, the chief is going to tell me how to make a traffic stop. Let me ask you, when the hell was the last time the chief made a traffic stop? Hell, he hasn't seen the ball since the kick-off."

"You think I'm making this shit up? Well, I'll tell you I've been at this agency for fifteen years—same circus, different clowns. I wouldn't trust these management assholes as far as I can throw them. I was talking to my lawyer yesterday, and he said, 'Document it, or better yet, get it on tape,' so when we take them to court this time, we'll stick it to them."

"I buy a lottery ticket every Friday, and I tell you what, if I hit the lottery, I'm going to pile all my police department bullshit on the front lawn of my house, and one of those pencil-necked assholes in the administration can come by and pick it up."

"The door ain't going to hit me in the ass. I mean it, you just watch, fifteen more years and I'm the hell out of here. I'll be gone. I'm getting the hell out of here."

Many officers can close their eyes and picture someone in their agency making these statements, maybe even themselves. Unfortunately, the orientation reflected in these statements can typify the second half of many law enforcement officers' careers. If you analyze each of the statements, the common theme is a belief that a wrong has been done to the officer by the agency, either at this time or at some time in the past. There is the continuing belief that the agency did something to injure the individual officer by violating some standard of ethical treatment or fair play. Although on occasion this is clearly the case, many times the officer's be-

Nobody, but nobody, will escape from a police career with their professional virginity intact.

liefs about having been victimized reflect only a generalized and paranoid distrust of everything and everybody in management and administrative roles. These statements, by some officers, say more about the respective officer's worldview of distrust than they do about whatever person, organization, or event on which they are commenting. Many officers, particularly those who have overidentified with the police role, can find themselves seeing the world from the viewpoint of victims of some poorly defined organizational conspiracy. They might do well to adapt some basic and overriding beliefs concerning a police career, such as the following basic truth:

Nobody, but nobody, will escape from a police career with their professional virginity intact. Everyone gets screwed by the agency at least one time.

Getting screwed does not mean being disciplined when an officer deserves to be disciplined. Getting screwed means officers receive the discipline—the letter of reprimand or days off without pay—when they really shouldn't have; or officers get transferred involuntarily when they are doing a good job; or they don't get the transfer or promotion that they deserve.

They got screwed.

Life Lessons

If you disagree with this premise, or want to know how to prepare for the potential injustice of a police career, go back to your respective agency, find one of the "big bosses," assume the position, and say "Do me, Do me, Do me." Get it over with and get over it. There is life after not getting the assignment you wanted or not getting the newer patrol car you thought you deserved. You know, the one that was manufactured just for you.

One can always see officers who don't understand this dynamic and who can't let it go. They are constantly upset with the agency over the wrongdoings or unfairness to which they have been subjected. They will recite a litany of wrongful acts committed by the chief, sheriff, or special agent in charge over the past fifteen or twenty years. They appear very focused on what wrong has been done to them and how they are totally untrusting of the agency. Have you ever noticed how these individuals appear consumed by the wrongful acts of the individuals running their agency? Stop and think about this for a moment. These officers have unwittingly fallen into the most common dilemma experienced by police officers. They do not understand how they have become trapped in this endless conflict with their own agency, and more important, they don't know how to get out of it. The only coping mechanisms they believe they have at their disposal don't work:

- They bitch about it.
- They file grievances.
- They file lawsuits.
- They quit the agency.
- They file stress disability claims.
- They orchestrate votes of "no confidence" against the chief.
- They say, "I don't give a damn anymore, and I ain't doing shit for this place anymore."

Although some of these strategies do have an appropriate time and place, none of them is going to provide officers with a capacity to understand their focused, all-consuming anger and rage at the agency. It is easy to determine which law enforcement officers in any agency have fallen prey to this dynamic. Usually it is the best officers, or at least the individuals who formerly were the best officers, the men and women victimized by the hypervigilance rollercoaster, those who unwittingly put the

Victims are defined as people who have control taken away from them.

rest of their lives on hold. They became twenty-six-hour-a-day police officers. The reality of being one-dimensional is that officers' sense of self is totally invested in a role they don't control. Ironically, those who do control the officers' role (and therefore the officer's sense of self) are the very people the officers have the least amount of trust or faith in—the administration or management of the agency. The more that officers focus on only their police role and become consumed by what has happened to them because of the agency, the more the overcommitted officers actually empower the very individuals they least trust. This can be where the previously idealistic and motivated officer begins thinking of herself or himself clearly as a victim. Victims are defined as people who have control taken away from them.

From Singular Identity to Victim

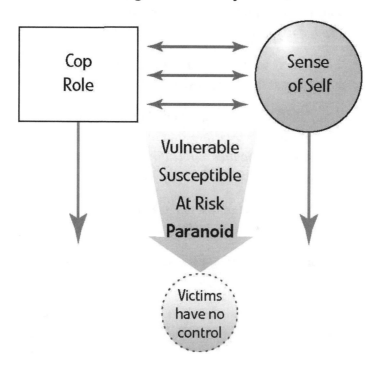

Victims Have No Control

Not only are officers thinking like victims, but they are thinking like paranoid victims. They have become overinvested emotionally in the police role and have made the police role the major element in their lives. Now, after being screwed by the agency in their mind, they realize they don't control their police role, and therefore they don't control the major element in their lives. Remember that possessing a sense of control over one's life, destiny, and sense of self is central to emotional well-being and psychological autonomy. To not control the major part of their lives is extremely unsettling for officers to experience. Officers experience intense and profound emotions when going through this dynamic:

"I can't stand being around these assholes."

"One of these days I'm going to get a chance to stick it to them, you just watch."

"I busted my ass working the streets for these people, and they just don't give a shit."

"I can't tell you how much time I have given this place without claiming overtime, and now they tag me for leaving fifteen minutes early and they're talking about giving me a day off without pay."

"I get so pissed off at this place, I just don't give a damn anymore about anything."

"I document everything I do and see around here. I play CYA big time."

"These assholes piss me off so much anymore that I can't get them out of my mind."

These officers are defining themselves as victims. This doesn't mean that the grievances they profess lack merit or didn't in fact take place; what the term *victim* means in this context is that they now wear their victim status as a badge of honor. They begin in some cases to obsess over the issue. Every so often a little bitching is probably good for the soul and psyche; however, becoming trapped in the victim role can be a career-ending experience, at least ending the positive contribution to the organization that the officer had likely made previously. Remember from the officer's orientation and worldview, the situation also has significant elements of distrust. The hypervigilance she or he learned on the streets to survive is now focused on surviving the internal organization.

"I can handle the assholes on the street; I just can't handle the assholes in management."

Case History

One exercise I enjoy doing while conducting training seminars in "Emotional Survival" is to ask a large audience of officers what their agency hat policy is. The most common response is that in most situations, it's optional to wear the hat except for certain formal occasions like promotional ceremonies or funerals. At this point I ask the class to imagine that I am now their chief of police and that immediately wearing hats is mandatory. "A hat will be worn every time officers step out of their car." (With state troopers the scenario is changed to taking the hats away from the troopers.) Needless to say, the emotional uproar this triggers within officers is amazing.

 "That's bullshit. The union is going to file suit on this."

continued

> *"You can't make me wear a hat. I'll get a doctor's note it causes migraines."*
>
> *"You say I have to wear a hat every time I step out of a car—fine, screw you, I won't step out of the car."*

The intensity of the responses are a measurement of the degree of emotional investment in the police role and the desire to gain control over the role. For some officers, a policy such as the mandatory wearing of hats would drive them off the deep end. Something as uneventful as a hat policy can put the emotionally overinvested officer into a full self-perceived victim role.

Officers *Do* Control Their Personal Lives

As discussed in chapter 4, the term *asshole* stems from the officer feeling in jeopardy or at risk from a person or location. Ironically, as the years of a police career pass, many officers feel most vulnerable and at risk when dealing with their own agencies. The reason for this feeling of vulnerability is that the agency controls the police role, and because of the long-term effect of the hypervigilance rollercoaster, the officer has long since abandoned the one realm where he or she has absolute control—the bottom half of the rollercoaster. Think about the rollercoaster shown below. An officer is getting all of her or his sense of self and feelings of accomplishment from the upper phase of the rollercoaster, but who controls the upper phase? The agency controls most of the events occurring in the upper phase. The agency controls policy, assignment, and operational priorities. Which phase does the officer control? The officer has absolute control of the lower phase of the rollercoaster, his or her personal life. But what if officers are doing nothing in the lower phase? What do they control? *They control nothing.*

Remember: Victims have no control.

The Hypervigilance Biological Rollercoaster®: Disengagement from Personal Life

On Duty **Overinvested**

Alive, Alert, Energetic, Involved, Humorous

Tired, Detached, Isolated, Apathetic

Off Duty **Underinvested**

The agency controls the upper phase of the rollercoaster (the police role).
The officer controls the lower phase of the rollercoaster (the personal life role).

Without training in emotional survival, the rollercoaster sets up officers to think, act, and live like victims, to not invest their energy, emotions, and sense of self in the phase of the rollercoaster that they do in fact control, the bottom, or off-duty, phase. It's a clear catch-22: Officers must maintain hypervigilance to perform and survive on the streets and practice good officer safety, yet it is this same hypervigilance that can cause officers to relinquish control of their personal lives. They cannot lower the upper phase of the rollercoaster. They *must* maintain the elevated physical state of heightened awareness of potential risk while functioning as officers. Without training and awareness of the rollercoaster, officers return home and experience the pendulum effect. The magic chair captures them. Weeks become months, and months become years across the span of a police career, as the "I usta" syndrome robs officers of any other interests or outlets. The good officers, the most enthusiastic officers, put all their energy and heartfelt commitment into one thing—trying to be the best cops they can be. Ironically, it is the nonpolice support systems that, when they remain intact, determine if the officers remain good cops for the duration of the entire police career—not good cops for just a few short years of high activity followed by fifteen or more years of perceiving themselves as victims and relinquishing their commitment to be the best cops they can be.

> *"I usta bust my ass for these people, but not anymore. I discovered a long time ago, the more you do, the more they screw with you. I pulled my horns in years ago. You never get in trouble for the traffic stop you didn't make."*

If officers continue to underinvest emotionally in the phase they actually control, they only intensify their victim status. By not addressing the bottom half of the rollercoaster and by trying to obtain all emotional and social needs from the on-duty phase, the police role, at the expense of strengthening the nonpolice roles, officers are in a trap. Without some assistance, they won't be able to get out. They don't know what is taking place in their lives emotionally. They spend all emotional energy trying to right the wrong they believe is causing their problems. Victim thinking has taken over their mindset. They are preoccupied with the issue at hand, with how they have been screwed. It is the last thing they think of every night and the first thing they think of every morning. It doesn't matter what the actual issue is that has become all-consuming in the officer's life because after a few years the issues change, but the victim-based thinking doesn't change.

Remember, these officers are not only thinking like victims, but they are thinking like paranoid victims. So if a friend or coworker attempts to ask these officers to "just let it go" or "move on with life," the officers will start recounting the wrongful acts perpetrated against them by the agency, and they won't accept the coworker's perspective. Further, victim officers will then feel the coworker has sold out to the agency and that they, the victim officers, are the only "true defenders of the faith." They are the only ones who have the courage to stand up and tell it like it is. They are blind to the fact that the world, as they see it, has become condensed to only one issue—their perceived victimization by the agency. This has become the officers' new worldview.

This is not in any way meant to imply that officers should become sheep and just accept unfairness or wrongful discipline.

If a grievance needs to be filed, file it.

If a lawsuit needs to be filed, file it.

Don't become consumed by it. Or, in the words of a veteran officer: "Don't let the assholes live in your head off duty rent-free."

Case History

Sergeant James is a sixteen-year veteran of the 1,200-officer department where he serves as a SWAT supervisor. The position Sgt. James maintains is a full-time special assignment. He has been a member of the SWAT team for twelve years, six of which have been as a supervisor. Sgt. James is well respected regionally for his expertise in SWAT-type tactical operations. He also instructs at regional, and on occasion national, tactical officer training courses. Sgt. James has received departmental citations for his performance while supervising numerous extremely intense SWAT operations. These past operations included his supervision of a multiple-hostage rescue operation, including a tactical entry under fire.

Sgt. James thoroughly enjoys his position as a SWAT supervisor and receives the respect of subordinates and supervisors alike. Although he maintains a good relationship with most personnel in his department, he has had an ongoing personality conflict, since his academy years, with one fellow officer. The individual whom Sgt. James has the conflict has recently been promoted to the rank of commander.

(continued)

After several transfers of other departmental command personnel have taken place, Sgt. James finds himself working directly under the supervision of the commander with whom he has the conflict. From Sgt. James's perspective, his role is one of professional expertise, and he relates that he has no problem working for anyone. He believes it is strictly a professional role, and any former personality conflicts are not important. The new commander, however, does not share Sgt. James's feelings on the issue of letting bygones be bygones and decides almost immediately upon taking command of SWAT that Sgt. James needs to be displaced from his position and returned to uniformed patrol as a patrol supervisor. Sgt. James has not worked in the field in a uniformed capacity for the past six years.

The commander also realizes that he cannot arbitrarily transfer Sgt. James from his position as a SWAT supervisor due to the exemplary service and performance that Sgt. James has maintained during his tenure in that assignment. The commander, realizing that he cannot directly and arbitrarily make the transfer occur, creates a new departmental policy requiring mandatory rotation of all special assignment supervisors every four years. The result of the commander's new policy is that Sgt. James is removed from SWAT team assignments and forced back into uniformed patrol. Sgt. James, who is typically a positive supervisor with an excellent attitude, becomes increasingly cynical toward the department. He becomes increasingly verbal about his beliefs: "The department screwed me and put me back on patrol, forgetting my twelve years of SWAT experience, just because the commander had it in for me."

In reviewing the case of Sgt. James, most veteran police officers can identify, from their own experience, an almost identical case. Clearly a dedicated and competent officer has experienced a major setback, professionally and personally. Sgt. James's future will be determined not by what the commander did to him but rather by how Sgt. James personally adjusts to the change. A victim would be able to view the situation and articulate how the agency screwed Sgt. James, that this is just another example of how the agency showed itself to be thankless and unappreciative of a competent and dedicated employee's years of contribution and service. It would be hard to argue that the victim perspective was without foundation, since in fact a petty and personally vindictive commander *did* screw Sgt. James. The real question would be: Is Sgt. James willing to remain a victim and focus on what he does not control, or does he want to become a survivor and focus on what he does control?

It's expected that Sgt. James will go through an adjustment period, holding hard feelings toward the agency, but what if the hard feelings don't subside? What if the hard feelings start becoming the way Sgt. James views every encounter he has with the agency? Depending on where the person is within the agency hierarchy when they view Sgt. James, they might draw different conclusions. A member of the management team seeing or hearing Sgt. James talk of his attitude toward the agency could form the conclusion that he is just another malcontent, some poorly performing employee who doesn't appreciate how good he has it. Someone viewing Sgt. James from the rank and file could draw the conclusion that Sgt. James is justified in how he feels toward the agency and is perfectly justified in doing as little as possible because "those unappreciative assholes in the administration screwed over another good cop."

Both perspectives are probably equally incorrect. The management perspective is not focusing on what is taking place personally for Sgt. James and is only viewing his behavior today. The rank-and-file individuals are not taking into consideration that Sgt. James has an obligation to provide competent police services to his agency, regardless of whether he agrees with the position to which he is presently assigned. Sgt. James, however, is the one left holding the bag emotionally. He is the one who has the emotional reactions to what has taken place in his life. He is the one who must emotionally balance the sense of loss of a position he highly valued. He also is the one who will have to balance the change in terms of how he views his entire police career. He can be a victim and go with that theme for the remainder of his career—many officers do. Or he can be a survivor and focus on the things he does control.

Victims focus on what they do not control.

Survivors focus on what they do control.

Sgt. James has several strategies available to him, some productive and some self-defeating. He could attempt to rationalize his lack of commitment and dedication to being back in patrol as a response to the way he has been treated by the agency. He could justify his minimal performance in his new position by stating, "If they don't care, why should I?" He could start a new career orientation of coasting and doing as little as possible or even become actively involved in attempting to undermine the agency administration and management.

These strategies are based on victim-based thinking. They involve considering the actions of individuals outside himself as the determining and responsible cause of his actions. This is the opposite of emotional self-determination. They involve focusing on what he does *not* control—the actions of others. For some people, who have been living their entire lives as self-perceived victims, this seems perfectly natural and rational.

> *"It is the commander's fault that Sgt. James has turned into a malcontent. If they hadn't transferred him, this never would have happened."*

This seems perfectly logical to the victim-based thinker. It means that other people determine Sgt. James's thinking and professional dedication; it is not Sgt. James's responsibility to control his own level of dedication and motivation. *If they hadn't transferred him, this never would have happened.* This is probably true, at least in part, but when would it have happened? The commander certainly is responsible for being a petty, vindictive, self-serving individual who abuses his professional authority to punish hard-working and dedicated police officers. He is without a doubt a poor manager and an even poorer example of a leader. Sgt. James, however, is responsible for his response to the transfer. A survivor orientation is necessary to adjust to this challenging situation. Waiting for the world, and particularly the world of a police officer, to change and be asshole-free is going to be a very long wait.

Good Cops Can Be as Overinvested as Malcontent Cops

Learning a survivor orientation is quite difficult, particularly if the officer has not been trained in the concepts of emotional overinvestment and has never heard of the hypervigilance rollercoaster. The first victims of the rollercoaster are the hard-working and dedicated police officers and their families. The second "victim" is the career itself. Officers who assume the victim orientation begin rationalizing and justifying to themselves behavior that they previously would have found unacceptable. Many people might encourage Sgt. James to back off caring at work. They might encourage him not to give a damn, but think about the actual effect that such behavior would have on Sgt. James and countless other good police officers in similar situations. It would mean they are rejecting their own internal core values of service and dedication. They would begin defining themselves as the opposite of what they previously stood for. They would begin defining themselves in oppositional or antagonistic terms to their previously held sense of self. Instead of being the twenty-six-hour-a-day police officers who love their role, they would become the twenty-six-hour-a-day officers who hate the job. Both are examples of significant overinvestment emotionally in a job or dimension of

Training Scenario

Often when instructing leadership courses to law enforcement executives, I will have some chief or other high-ranking individual discussing a case example at their respective agency and relate:

Chief: This guy I have is a real malcontent. He doesn't give a shit about anything. He bitches about everything going on at work. He couldn't care less about the job of being a cop

Author: Chief, your guy doesn't give a shit about being a cop?

Chief: Yeah, he couldn't care less. He bitches about everything going on at work

Author: Chief, I wonder if you could give me one example where you ever bitched about something that you didn't give a shit about. Bitching is actually a form of giving a shit. You don't bitch about stuff you don't care about

It's hard from some law enforcement executive personnel to appreciate that many times the malcontent employee is the most emotionally overinvested officer. It's just that he or she is investing negative energy into the self-perceived victim role.

their lives they do not control. The only difference between the two orientations is that one maintains a positive charge emotionally and the other a negative charge.

Malcontent officers are defining their lives by the job role as much as positive, pro-agency, enthusiastic officers are. Malcontents define themselves by taking the opposite orientation or position to how the job is defined by the organization. Whether positive or negative overinvestment, the officers are allowing their sense of self to be defined by individuals other than themselves.

In both cases, this orientation enables victim-based thinking to thrive. Malcontent officers also have a somewhat self-destructive orientation because they now reject the very core values of commitment and enthusiasm that were previously central to their own self-definition. That our best officers are most affected illustrates why teaching officers how to become emotional survivors needs to be a high priority in law enforcement training; unfortunately, it is rarely, if ever, a subject of importance to either organizations or individual officers.

Victim-Based Thinking

What happens if the victim orientation becomes the predominant way of viewing the world for Sgt. James and countless other law enforcement officers who, from their perspective, have been screwed by the agency? What if they begin seeing all events in their lives as affected or colored by the treatment they received from the organization? What happens if all decisions these officers are required to make are potentially contaminated by a "victim tint"? Do police officers potentially compromise their professionalism and integrity when they define themselves as victims?

If you ask people the question, "What do victims want?" you will hear a variety of answers:

- restitution
- fairness
- righting the wrong done to them
- retribution

All these terms are basically a more socially acceptable way of expressing our desire for revenge or payback. What each of these desires involves is a manner of taking back control that has been taken away by the offending party. In the criminal justice system, each of these concepts is particularly important when a genuine victim has been violated. This is the reason *real* victims have a chance to speak at criminal-sentencing hearings, and the reason juries award damages to real victims in civil court claims.

What about the *self-perceived* victim in the workplace who wants to recover or take back an intangible, such as enthusiasm or dedication? This is particularly difficult because what these people want to recover—motivation, enthusiasm, and idealism about the job—are in reality in their control to begin with. It is not the person transferring Sgt. James who controls the sergeant's motivation and idealism. Sgt. James controls that. The commander controls only the assignment; Sgt. James controls his emotional reaction to the assignment.

Some individuals in law enforcement, once they become self-perceived victims, can cease investing in the work role many years before they retire or leave. Once officers see themselves as having been victimized, it can be hard to let it go and return to enthusiastic and committed work, particularly if the offending commander is still present in the organization. Without assistance or insight into the dynamics of malcontentism and overinvestment, these officers potentially begin a predictable system of thinking that can start guiding their judgment and behavior. When officers begin seeing themselves as victims, they begin possessing many of the clearly identifiable attributes listed in the box below.

Victim Attributes

- merging of personal and professional roles
- hypersensitivity to change (all change is a personal assault)
- rigidity and inflexibility
- ever-present feeling of threat from the organization
- belief one is being controlled or persecuted by the agency
- need to retaliate against management hierarchy for perceived wrongs
- social isolation from others in the organization except a few "true believers"

- grandiose sense of self-importance: "I'm one of the best cops in this department"
- exaggerated perception of past accomplishments
- internalized sense of entitlement

Unfortunately, the above list of attributes paints a picture of a person who has lost the way. Many good police officers possess many of the above traits. They may also report a generalized feeling of being caught in a world where they cannot escape—the ever-present emotions these attributes create.

Entitlement

Of the traits listed above, one of the most damaging to law enforcement officers and agencies alike is the internalized sense of entitlement. A belief in entitlement can begin driving an officer's decision making. This belief can be explained as an occupationally acquired worldview that because of everything police officers have to put up with, all the B.S., they deserve a break. The foundation of entitlement orientation is in victim-based thinking. Entitlement can permit the officers and agencies to rationalize behavior they would not normally engage in and see it as perfectly acceptable. Victim-based thinking also lets the officers blame others or externalize responsibility for their own behavior. To illustrate this point, you might ask a group of officers the following question:

> *"How many of you think it is acceptable to go out in the parking garage, select a car someone personally owns, take your car key out, and put a key scratch or gouge down the entire length of the car?"*

The obvious response from the officers will be that the behavior is unacceptable. It is not appropriate to vandalize someone's car. When you ask why this isn't right to do, you'll receive several answers:

- "It is morally wrong."
- "It is unlawful."
- "I wasn't raised that way."
- "I don't do stuff like that."
- "We arrest people who do stuff like that."
- "You could get cited or arrested."
- "You could get fired."
- "I wouldn't want anyone to do that to me."

Each officer sees that damaging another person's property is unacceptable, inappropriate, and clearly criminal behavior. If you present a slightly different scenario, however, the answers can change:

> *"You go out in the parking garage, and you find a large scratch or key gouge in your personal car, and you ask, "Who did this?" and several of your friends come forward and identify the person who damaged your car. Would it be easier now to go put a key scratch or gouge in the car belonging to the person who scratched your car?"*

> *Some folks may say, "Two wrongs don't make a right," but most responses will be along the following lines:*

> *"I'd scratch his car right after I kicked his butt."*

In one situation, scratching the car is wrong, but when a perception of having been victimized is injected, the response changes. The experience or perception of having been victimized changes the rules for many individuals:

An eye for an eye

A tooth for a tooth

A paint job for a paint job

Because many law enforcement officers have not received even basic training in emotional survival, they develop the worldview of having been victimized. The hypervigilance rollercoaster and "I usta" syndrome have taken their toll, and the officer can begin living life as an emotionally overinvested, self-perceived victim.

Situational versus Core Values

What can happen to officers whose worldview is tainted, maybe even consumed, by this belief of having been victimized? Considering the propensity for some politicians and the media for placing blame on police officers for every social inequity in our society, cops feeling "victimized" is not a rare event. How does it affect the officers who each day are still required to perform their professional duties under emotionally demanding and, at times, physically threatening situations? How does the lack of an emotional survival orientation and skill set affect officers who must face the daily requirement of making a full range of decisions that can demand the wisdom of Solomon? Remember also, Solomon was not making his decisions with cellphone cameras jammed into his face while he wears a bodycam.

The decisions law enforcement officers are required to make demand individuals who are emotionally balanced and are not perceptually tainted by a victim orientation. Permitting law enforcement officers to make decisions from a victim perspective without benefit of emotional survival awareness is grossly unfair to law enforcement officers themselves and to the public they serve. The victim orientation robs the officer of the benefit of using a lifetime of internalized core values as the foundation for decision making. The *core values* become *situational values.*

The movement from core values to situational values, based on a belief of having been victimized, permits officers to rationalize behavior they previously would not have accepted in themselves. It also permits the officers to project blame for their own behavior onto other persons.

"If that guy didn't want his car scratched, he shouldn't have scratched mine."

"If they wanted Sgt. James to remain a dedicated officer, they should have left him in SWAT and not screwed with him."

At first glance, these statements seem logical enough because there is a factual basis for having been wronged and violated. On further examination, however, these statements are just another example of the contaminated thinking police officers hear each day on the street:

- "He called me a name. That's why I shot him."
- "He cut me off in traffic. That's why I ran into the back of his car."
- "She was messing around with my man. That's why I stabbed her."
- "He was talking trash to me. That's why I kicked his ass."
- "She owed me ten dollars. That's why I messed up her car."
- "They were playing the music real loud. That's why I threw the rock at their window."
- "He was on our turf. That's why we capped him."

And on and on and on and on *ad nauseam.* Basically, these people are saying, "It's the other person's fault how I behaved. After all, I can't be expected to be a responsible person who is held accountable for my own behavior. I'm entitled to do what I did."

This is the basic paradigm of victim-based entitlement thinking:

"They screwed with me, which is why I engaged in this behavior."

"The rules don't apply to me because of what I had to put up with."

You would think police officers would be highly sensitive to the reasoning of people who abdicate responsibility for their own behavior using pathological excuse mongering. Every day officers must listen to the dregs of society using self-perceived victim rationalizations as an excuse not to be held accountable for a wide spectrum of outrageous, even criminal, behavior. Possibly the daily exposure of police officers to individuals who refuse to accept responsibility for their own actions provides victim-based-thinking officers a paradigm for rationalizing inappropriate behavior. They can then utilize this paradigm to justify their own professional misdeeds as officers.

"The chief did_____. That's why I did_____."

"I got screwed by this department when they_____. That's why I did_____."

The thinking is clearly victim based because it projects accountability onto something the officer doesn't control—the behavior of the perceived offender. The tragedy in not addressing this type of thinking through emotional survival training and intervention is that it can ruin the careers and lives of many good police officers. By not providing training in emotional survival so that police officers can clearly see the difference between self-perceived victims and emotional survivors, law enforcement organizations don't give officers the ability to maintain their most valued asset: their core values. At the same time the officers are losing their most valued assets, the

Good officers do not show their victim status by going out and doing something wrong. They go out and stop doing something right.

organizations themselves are losing their most valuable assets, the ethical and emotional stable foundation of police officers.

This failure of adequate career preparation allows officers to justify their behavior against a standard of situational values. It basically sets up the officers for failure and devastation in their personal *and* professional lives. Organizations are also set up to fail when they comprise cadres of officers who perceive themselves as having been victimized by the organization. Leadership requires "ethical followership." When victim-based thinking and entitlement take over officers' worldviews, they can progress down a predictable path of inappropriate behavior patterns.

Acts of Omission
Good officers do not show their victim status by going out and doing something wrong. They go out and stop doing something right. Officers initially show they are self-perceived victims by lowering their levels of production, their standard for professional duties. Self-initiated activities, such as traffic citations, reduce. Officers justify the nonperformance of job duties based on their self-perception of having been victimized by the agency. They begin engaging in acts of omission.

> ❝ *"If they don't care, why should I?"*
>
> *"You never get in trouble for the stop you don't make."*
>
> *"I answer my calls. That's all I get paid to do!"* ❞

At first, it might seem like acts of omission of professional duties are not a major worry for the individual officer but rather a production problem for the agency. But these acts are very much a problem for both officer *and* agency. When the officer can rationalize any wrongdoing, whether by omission of duties or by active engagement in wrongdoing, the officer is violating his or her own core values and beginning a journey down a path that can have both personal and professional ramifications. Enthusiasm is replaced by diffuse anger. The active go-getter officer of a few years ago can become the officer who sees nothing and hears nothing and does nothing. Officers justify and rationalize all this behavior because of the violation done to them by the agency years ago. Some entire law enforcement agencies operate as a subculture of victim-based entitlement thinkers, which provides significant peer support for the nonperformance of duties. Acts of omission can be demonstrated by the following case example.

Case History

Officer Kerri Smith is a nine-year veteran officer of a medium-size sheriff's department. Her entire career to date has been in uniformed street patrol. The agency at which she works also maintains a large county jail and requires all officers to rotate to the jail for two-year tours-of-duty during their careers. Officer Smith has just received her notice of being rotated to perform her jail tour on the next scheduled shift change in ninety days. (Her agency gives the ninety-day rotation notice to permit officers ample time to arrange personal issues, such as childcare, because the jail uses a different shift-rotation format than the patrol division uses.) Officer Smith, who is an active street officer, thinks placing experienced officers in a detention capacity is both a poor management strategy and a waste of good police officers' street experience. She approaches the chief and attempts to argue against her having to do the mandatory jail rotation, telling the chief "the department should hire animal control officers to work with the assholes in the jail and leave the good officers on the street, so they can keep the jail full by doing good police work." The chief informs Officer Smith that he doesn't particularly care if Smith thinks the policy is appropriate or fair and tells her "'Fair' is what you pay to ride on the bus." The chief clearly informs Officer Smith that she can expect to be rotated to the jail in ninety days as planned. (continued)

Officer Smith, realizing she will rotate to the jail in ninety days no matter what she says or does, ceases doing any self-initiated street police work during the time her rotation is pending. She regularly sees traffic violations occur in her presence and takes no enforcement action. On calls for service to which she is dispatched, she rarely makes an arrest, and her officer reports are little more than one- or two-line summaries of what has taken place. She only minimally conducts investigations and generally has ceased working as a police officer. Her supervisor on several occasions has called her on the radio and Officer Smith has failed to respond, telling the supervisor she didn't hear the radio transmission, when in fact she did hear the transmission and just refused to answer. She tells her fellow officers:

"Screw the department. If they want me to be a jailer for two years, why should I act like a street cop?"

Officer Smith certainly sees herself as having been victimized by the agency at which she has worked for nine years. She certainly can gain professional agreement from many law enforcement professionals about her negative thoughts on using experienced street officers in the jail. She would probably gain agreement that the chief was harsh and insensitive in speaking to an experienced officer in the manner he spoke to Officer Smith. She could also obtain agreement that the chief was following a foolish personnel strategy in the jail-rotation policy. Although the chief is clearly responsible for poor leadership and possibly poor personnel practices, who in reality is responsible for Officer Smith's lack of performance of her police duties on the street during the ninety days prior to her jail rotation?

If Officer Smith is waiting for a time in her career when she will be free of foolish departmental policies, she might have a long wait. It is quite understandable that she would be highly disappointed in her transfer to the jail. It is also quite understandable that she feels the transfer policy is an example of poor police personnel management, but how does she get past the reality of the transfer? Although she is not able to change the transfer itself, is Officer Smith helpless to overcome the emotional reaction to her situation? Are the acts of omission that Officer Smith is engaging in destructive only to the overall productivity of the agency? How are her actions and change of heart affecting Officer Smith herself? What are the effects on Officer Smith of daily violating her own core values of dedicated service and professional enthusiasm? Does engaging in a work orientation that is directly opposite to how she has worked for the past nine years affect Officer Smith personally?

By violating her own core values, because she believes she has been victimized, Officer Smith is actually doing harm to herself and her own sense of self-esteem. Although it is easy to blame the agency, the chief, or a personnel rotation policy, Officer Smith is acting like a self-perceived victim and is beginning to self-destruct. She sees herself daily permit traffic violators to avoid citations. She is invalidating, in her own eyes, the importance and significance of the past nine years of admirable police service that has typified her career. Her victim-based assessment of what has happened to her permits her to say events outside of her control are causing the change in her professional orientation.

She can begin seeing herself not as a free-standing professional law enforcement officer, but as merely a puppet whose professional demeanor is controlled by others. Clearly others control the assignment, but who controls Officer Smith's professional demeanor? She thinks everything is out of her control:

> *"I am not responsible for my own demeanor, values, enthusiasm, and integrity. Someone else controls that."*

The irony and paradox of this type of thinking is that it actually empowers, in the officer's mind, the very individuals who have caused the professional setback. If Officer Smith acknowledges her extreme disappointment in the transfer to the jail and respectfully expresses her belief that the jail transfer policy is inappropriate and archaic, yet continues to be a productive street police officer, several things will likely happen. She will still do her two years in the jail whether she likes it or not, yet she will be able to retain her orientation that she controls her sense of self and professional demeanor. She will be focusing on what she values and what she controls, which is being an effective and dedicated police officer.

Some officers could confuse the issue of what Officer Smith really controls and say, "She was demonstrating what she controlled by not being productive. She controls her self-initiated activity level." Although she does control her self-initiated activity level, by engaging in acts of omission, she is violating her own core values and damaging her sense of self-esteem as an officer and a person. Officer Smith is also violating an oath of office she took as a police officer.

Officer Smith's acts of omission only reinforce and further her worldview of herself as a victim, not as a survivor. A survivor might say:

> *"I hate the thought of working in the jail for two years. I think it is a totally inappropriate policy, and the department should hire animal control officers to deal with the assholes in the jail, but I have always done as good a job as I can as an officer, and I will do as good a job as I can in there and count my days until I can get back on the street."*

This is not just a strategy of being a good employee; it is a strategy to focus on your core values and realize that you, not the agency or organizational administration, are in control of your own behavior and demeanor. This survival strategy would permit Officer Smith to dislike the assignment but keep her core values and orientation as a survivor intact. Victims unfortunately begin acting like victims in all phases of their lives, and something such as a transfer can precipitate into a series of cascading actions that ruin lives and careers, as, unfortunately, happened with Officer Smith.

Case History

As Officer Smith's case unfolds, she begins developing her victim orientation aggressively during the ninety days prior to her rotation. She announces that almost everything that has come out of the "head shed," or administration, is "bullshit." Her productivity is down, and she is no longer the enthusiastic officer she had been throughout her nine-year career. She dreads the thought of going into the jail for several reasons. She detests the nature of the work involved in being a jail officer, but she realizes she still misses the camaraderie and social networking that has been part of her work experience up to this point. Her only friends are her coworkers on the street.

Officer Smith is also a typical officer who has never given any significant thought to her own emotional survival strategies. She has never understood its importance and has received no training in the concepts of the hypervigilance rollercoaster or being emotionally overinvested in the job at the expense of other support systems. She begins her jail rotation resentful, angry, and uncooperative with her new supervisors and coworkers. She particularly dislikes those officers who have volunteered to remain in the jail bureau after their mandatory two-year rotation, calling them "lifers" and "losers." She finds the duties of being a jail officer "little more than babysitting assholes." As the months inside the jail pass, Officer Smith finds herself increasingly moody in her personal life. She works her shift at the jail and returns to her home, watches television, and generally is captured by the magic chair. Every day becomes a cycle of work and a sedentary off-duty lifestyle.

Approximately six months after beginning her rotation into the jail (or "zoo," as Officer Smith calls it), she is assigned to work as a booking officer, handling incoming prisoners. This position can be particularly provocative and confrontational in the jail because it is the point where

(continued)

arresting officers process inmates and transfer custody to the jail division. It is the scene of numerous physical confrontations.

Shortly after starting this new position, Officer Smith is taking custody of an inmate from three arresting street officers, all of whom have already completed their two-year mandatory jail rotation, when they begin ribbing Officer Smith about doing her "turn in the barrel" (her jail rotation). When Officer Smith states, "My tour as a babysitter for assholes is 25 percent over," the arrestee, not appreciating the comment about "assholes," tells Officer Smith that the "only assholes around this place are the ones with badges." Officer Smith, in the presence of the other officers, punches the prisoner and slams the prisoner's head against the wall, telling her to "shut her mouth or I'll shut it for you." The prisoner complies with Officer Smith's demand, but through her public defender, she files an internal affairs complaint and a civil lawsuit against Officer Smith for brutality.

The booking desk of the jail, due to its provocative and confrontational location, is one of the departmental locations where all officer-inmate interactions are video-taped by an openly displayed surveillance camera. The videotape clearly shows Officer Smith striking the hand-cuffed prisoner without any signs of physical threat from the prisoner that would warrant such physical actions in defense by Officer Smith. Officer Smith is terminated from employment for her actions and is charged with assault and civil rights violation by the prosecutor's office. Officer Smith, being charged with a criminal act, is required to financially fund her own legal defense, and because of the videotaped evidence against her, she is forced to accept a plea agreement for assault. Although she is not required by her plea agreement to do jail time, she is convicted of a crime and is decertified by her state P.O.S.T. as a peace officer, thus ending a law enforcement career and losing a retirement package that she was only eleven years from earning. She ultimately loses her home due to loss of income. If you ask Officer Smith how all this happened in a matter of a few months, she will gladly tell you:

"It was the fault of the chief and his damned jail-rotation policy."

"It was the fault of the assholes in the jail."

"It was the fault of the damned Big Brother snitch cameras."

Acts of Commission

Officer Smith's story points out the tragedies that can befall good officers once they become obsessed with a victim-based thinking orientation. Acts of *omission* yield to acts of *commission*. The continuum passes from passive avoidance of duties due to the belief of having been victimized to the active commission of rule violations. First, the officer breaks or ignores administrative rules; ultimately, criminal violations can occur. Officer Smith was a good cop. She just didn't have a clue about emotional survival nor her developing victim orientation. Her anger kept feeding on itself until she began acting in ways that had not typified her behavior previously. Officer Smith did not have a record or reputation of being heavy handed or physically aggressive while working for nine years on the street.

Here again victim-based thinkers would point to the jail-rotation policy and say it was to blame, that Officer Smith was not responsible for her behavior.

"They shouldn't put good cops into that hell hole."

They would blame the organization, after the fact, but would not have provided Officer Smith any upfront strategies to survive the jail rotation and preserve her career. Wouldn't it have been far better if Officer Smith had a strategy of emotional survival that would have permitted her to overcome the two-year rotation in the jail and see it as little more than a bad *temporary* assignment instead of a life-changing and career-ending event?

The nine years of good police work and the hypervigilance rollercoaster set up Officer Smith to be underinvested in activities away from work. Her role of "street police officer" was foremost in her world—the rollercoaster had taken another victim. To add insult to injury, Officer Smith also had to realize that her friends, who were the arresting officers of the prisoner she assaulted, also received significant disciplinary action partly due to Officer Smith's behavior. The videotape clearly showed that the arresting officers witnessed the assault and failed to restrain Officer Smith and failed to report the incident to their supervisors. In this case, victim thinking made decisions along the lines of "loyalty versus integrity," a difficult choice for officers to make. Loyalty and integrity are the two cornerstones of effective and ethical law enforcement. The victim, however, forgets loyalty *and* integrity and begins viewing the world as loyalty *versus* integrity. As an individual's sense of self begins to get battered, the need for group and peer acceptance and approval increases. Tragically, many victim officers value loyalty to fellow officers far more than integrity and honesty.

What could Officer Smith have done when she found out she was no longer going to be working in uniformed patrol, but assigned to the jail for twenty-four months? What can Sgt. James do now that he is out of SWAT and back in uniformed patrol? It is interesting to see that one officer was a victim because he was being sent back to uniformed patrol, and one officer was a victim because she was being taken out of uniformed patrol. Two good officers with lots of *street* survival skills but no *emotional* survival skills, both faced a career-defining decision. Could the outcome have been different in Officer Smith's case? Could she have been trained to be an emotional survivor and still be on the job, waiting until she had "done her time in the barrel" to get back on the street as an officer? Back to her career and constructive service to her community, herself, and her family? The answer is clearly yes, but how could she have done it? How could these officers have become emotional survivors?

How to Become an Emotional Survivor

What are the attributes of emotional survivors? In all the case histories in previous chapters, the officers appear to have one thing in common: The orientation of dedication that started and typified the beginning of their law enforcement careers and that somehow, across the course of time, became derailed. All the officers started out idealistic, committed, and enthusiastic as they began the journey across the law enforcement years, but they all found themselves becoming embittered, angry, and disillusioned. Officer Smith's termination after being transferred to the jail division demonstrates an officer suffering significant emotional and economic loss due to a worldview that she learned, internalized, and was rewarded for as a police officer. All the officers, ironically, had in common the orientation and worldview that their police career was central to their lives, and unfortunately, this same career became a pivotal point of loss for each of them. None of the victim officers appeared to learn how to establish a balanced emotional investment portfolio.

Could these officers have retained across the span of a police career the idealism, enthusiasm, and motivation that typified their earlier years? If the officers understood emotional survival even remotely as well as they understood tactical skills, investigative skills, or street survival, they would have likely not fallen prey to the overwhelming orientation of victim-based thinking. As survivors, they would

A much more helpful approach for the officer leaving work is to have the goal of not so much turning off police work as turning on something different.

have focused on the events that they personally could control. The officers would clearly know the difference between things that they do not control and things that they do. This would not be a superficial Pollyanna outlook on life. It would not be a "don't worry, be happy" worldview. It would take work and dedication to be the best and safest law enforcement officer that each of them had the potential of being and then be able each day to turn it off and become the best fly fisherman, the best grad student, the best weightlifter, the best marathon runner, the best little league coach, the best whatever the cop wants to be. Of course, it is much easier said than done to truly *leave* police work each day due to the overwhelming impact of hypervigilance and the biological rollercoaster dropping the officer into that parasympathetic detached and depressed state at day's end.

A much more helpful approach for the officer leaving work is to have the goal of not so much turning off police work as *turning on* something different. The case histories in this book can typify what happens to many good law enforcement officers—everything in life becomes an "I usta." One way not to go down that road is for officers early in their careers to be trained in what it takes to maintain a sense of control in their personal lives. Training would need to take place not just with the officers but also with the officers' family members. At the beginning stages of an officer's career, this could be a parent; later on, a significant other or spouse and even children could be incorporated in the training.

Survivors Practice Aggressive Personal Time Management and Goal Setting

Over the years I have interviewed law enforcement personnel at the point of their retirement from police work, asking a series of questions about how the officers viewed their career. One question I asked of each soon-to-be-retired law enforcement professional was "Looking back on your career, do you have any regrets?" By far the most frequently obtained response has been

> *"I wish I had taken the time to do more things with my kids when they were young."*

The concept of lost time from their personal lives was the predominant theme of regret. Yet very rarely are law enforcement officers taught any skill development in personal time management. It is not seen as a relevant concept for preserving and maintaining a committed idealistic law enforcement workforce. The relationship between on-duty performance and off-duty quality of life is lost. Much lip service is given to the concept of work-life balance, but very few skills to accomplish it are actually taught. Even fewer management practices encourage the concept.

How do you teach officers to be emotional survivors? The first step clearly is to teach officers to maintain control of their personal lives. Taking and maintaining control of one's personal life sounds like such a basic concept that it should go without saying. In reality, however, one of the first dimensions of control law enforcement officers lose is the day-to-day sense of being in charge of a schedule, of being able to control personal time. The ability to self-initiate proactive control of activities, priorities, and schedules seems to disappear from officers' day-to-day experience quite soon after they become members of the law enforcement agency. The everyday real-time demands of the profession, plus the biological rollercoaster, push personal time to the back burner; it becomes of secondary importance and takes place only in the depressive downside of the rollercoaster. Such things as changing work shifts, training schedules, exigent operational needs, forced overtime, and court subpoenas take away so much of a law enforcement officer's day-to-day life and available personal time.

With today's overwhelming number of intrusive digital communication devices cutting into limited personal time, it is hard to establish a clear boundary between professional world and personal world. They potentially blur together. The electronic digital leash is hard for many committed law enforcement professionals to shed. It's easy for an officer to start developing the victim orientation. The biological rollercoaster drops the off-duty officer into the depression state, and activities they actually control slip away into "I ustas."

> **Victim Orientation (Does Not Control)**
> "I have no control over my on-duty time. The job pretty much dictates what my days off and work schedules are going to be" combines with "I have no control over my off-duty personal time; the job has just taken over."
>
> **Survivor Orientation (Does Control)**
> "I don't control a lot of what happen on duty, but I need to be in charge of my daily scheduling of personal time and goal setting to every extent possible."

Survivors, unlike victims, have a clear sense of personal time control. Survivors develop and continually use a specific and practical technique of personal time management, a strategy that permits them to harness the available time in their personal lives to accomplish whatever goals they choose to pursue. Teaching the development and use of a specific personal time-management technique is an extremely important need for police officers for two strong reasons.

The Law Enforcement Profession Operates 24/7

First, police work, by its very nature, is terribly intrusive into an individual's personal life. It's not an 8-to-5, Monday-through-Friday experience. Police agencies are 24/7, and without specific training in the subject of emotional survival, many young officers, caught up in the enthusiasm and excitement of the early career years, begin living their own lives as if their individual police role were also 24/7. The early career years of many young officers prove that the job requires working many hours beyond the typical forty-hour work week, and many profess, "There is nothing I can do about it." The victim mindset begins: "Time is out of my control." This is also fertile ground for the belief that "a personal life is an unnecessary luxury."

*"Why do I need a personal life? I love being a cop, and
going on duty seems more like fun than work."*

—a three-year cop

As any veteran cop will tell you, it will not be many years before
the orientation and belief of that three-year cop changes. Teaching
officers from the absolute beginning of their careers to be aggressive personal time managers and goal setters is essential.

Police Work Destroys Spontaneity

The second major reason to train law enforcement officers in aggressive time control, or proactivity in their view of their personal
time, is that they lose any sense of spontaneity in personal activities because of the biological rollercoaster. The rollercoaster drops
them into that depressive-like state and robs law enforcement personnel of all spontaneity and enthusiasm after the workday has
ended. They are exhausted.

Coming home from work each day and riding the magic chair
leaves officers with a view of personal time that is less than self-directed. Officers can spend the limited hours of their personal lives
surfing the internet, scrolling social media, playing video games, or
staring at a television set, letting life pass them by. In many ways,
the officer at home, sit-
ting in the magic chair,
is acting basically like a
passive recipient victim
of whatever information,
entertainment, or total
nonsense the internet or
television world is send-

> *Officers can spend the limited
> hours of their personal lives
> surfing the internet, scrolling
> social media, playing video games,
> or staring at a television set,
> letting life pass them by.*

ing forth. This time spent in the magic chair is the beginning of a
passive orientation toward personal time management. It doesn't
take planning, it doesn't take goal setting, it doesn't take grabbing
control of personal time. It doesn't take self-determination and
self-responsibility. Actually it doesn't take anything. It's the basic
no-brainer—just stare at the smart phone, click the TV remote

control, turn on the computer and check out. The officer begins having a passive reactive orientation toward the world of her or his personal life.

Training Scenario

During my law enforcement career, I was sent along with four other agency members to a "Time Management" training session hosted at the training center of a national technology company. All five law enforcement attendees thought the training was "bullshit," but we obviously complied and attended. Upon arrival at the tech company training site, we discovered that all other attendees at the seminar were technology professionals from the company that was hosting us, their five law enforcement "guests." From the outset of the training, it became apparent that the high-tech folks lived in a different professional world than we did as law enforcement officers—we all felt like fish out of water. The instructor began the training session by asking each attendee what technique they currently used to manage their work project time. Each technology professional gladly articulated their individual time-management strategies, including ranking projects in order of importance or by due dates. Each demonstrated their proactive approach to managing their work project schedules. As the instructor moved around the classroom, asking each attendee about his or her individual time-management practices, it was soon our turn (we were obviously all sitting in the back row of the classroom). The first and most verbal of my law enforcement colleagues looked at the technology instructor and stated:

"We're all cops. We show up to work, shit happens, and we handle it."

The instructor stopped and looked bewildered. He didn't understand the response, especially considering that each of the technology professionals had gone into great detail on how they planned out each day's work project, even on occasion planning the next day's work in advance. The cop's response was an alien concept to the instructor, who verbally stated, "I don't understand." My law enforcement colleague reiterated his reply:

> *"We're all cops. We show up to work, shit happens, and we handle it."*

The "Time Management" instructor, who obviously dealt with a different work population of people who could proactively schedule their work, was intrigued by the cop's answer and stated: "Well, just how do you know that this 'shit' is happening?" The cop continued, in his typical communication style:

> *"We have a little box in our police cars, and a voice comes out of the box and tells us what the shit is that's happening and where it is happening. We drive there, and we handle the shit."*

Needless to say, the instructor was intrigued by the five law enforcement guests who represented an entirely different work universe then he was accustomed to interacting with. The instructor further inquired, "You mean to say that each day when you show up to work, you have no idea what you might be doing on that particular day? You mean your work is purely reactive?" The cop replied, "Yeah, that's why we are called first responders. . . . We respond." The instructor commented, "I don't know anyone like you folks," to which the cop replied "Well, I don't know anyone like you folks either."

On duty is reactive. The cop must learn to develop a proactive off-duty personal orientation.

Proactive versus Reactive

The expertise of good law enforcement professionals begins in the reactive phase. Someone dials 911, or the investigator is handed a case, and law enforcement responds. It's not hard to understand how law enforcement officers lose their sense of being in charge of their personal time. First, because of the physiology of hypervigilance, then because of the rather demanding and controlling interference in their personal lives by the work schedule, law enforcement officers from their earliest years on the force learn to surrender any sense of proactivity. The time-management instructor in the training scenario above came from a different universe.

Police work requires an on-duty *reactive* orientation for public safety as opposed to a *proactive* orientation. This reactive orientation is best understood in thinking about what many law enforcement officers do each day at work, particularly during the early stages of their careers. Uniformed police officers in a patrol capacity basically drive around the streets of their jurisdiction and wait for something to happen. They wait for calls for service. Although community policing has a goal of having officers become more proactive in their orientation toward the police role, it will never reduce the innate reactivity of police work. Citizens will always have a need to dial 911 and have public safety professionals arrive to serve and protect them. Law enforcement officers learn early on in their career that so much of police work is having a worldview of intense observation and being ready to react.

This reactive orientation is effective for being prepared to respond when events unfold in the professional life of the law enforcement officer. A reactive orientation is tragically inadequate, however, when it becomes the officer's worldview in his or her personal life. It's a different state of affairs to operate a patrol car as a police officer and wait for an event to take place or a call to be dispatched than it is to plan an activity with family or schedule time for physical fitness or recreation. On-duty officers learn to see the world from the reactive perspective as a means of increasing survival through hypervigilance and increased officer safety. Then they return home and attempt to continue being reactive, but there is typically nothing intense to react to, hence the feeling of letdown. So, unfortunately, some officers reactively ride the magic chair into a life of "I ustas."

A reactive orientation, which is essential for street survival, can be lethal to a personal relationship. Officers need to appreciate the requirement of reactivity on duty but balance this with proactivity off duty. It is extremely difficult to make the transition from reactivity to proactivity due to the emotional and physical letdown of hypervigilance. What do they feel like doing after work? Nothing! What will they probably do after work? Nothing! When a person feels like doing nothing, they probably will do nothing.

Officers can determine if they are falling into the reactive mode at home by reviewing their decision-making strategies to see if they are using a reactive time orientation in their personal lives. Obviously, the reactive orientation that's appropriate in their professional lives does have shortcomings when used in their personal lives.

Are You a Reactive Decision Maker?

Imagine it is your Friday evening. The workday has ended, and you've just walked in the door from work and are beginning your weekend. Does the following conversation sound familiar? If so, you are a reactive decision maker.

Officer: I don't feel like cooking, do you?

Significant
other: No. I don't feel like cooking either.

Officer: Do you feel like going out to get a bite to eat?

Significant Sure. That sounds good. Where do you want to
other: go?

Officer: Oh, I don't know. Any place is okay with me.

Significant Well, what do you feel like eating? Would you like
other: Mexican food, Italian food, seafood? What sounds
good?

Officer: Oh, I don't know. I don't care. Anything you want
is okay with me. It's your call.

Significant other:	Well, I don't know. Help me out. What would you like?
Officer:	Look, I don't know. I've been making decisions all week. Anything's fine with me.
Significant other:	Well, where do you want to go?
Officer:	Where do you want to go?
Significant other:	Where do you want to go?
Officer:	Where do you want to go?
Significant other:	Where do you want to go?
Officer:	Where do you want to go?
Significant other:	Where do you want to go?

Does the above dialogue exchange sound familiar? This is a perfect example of a law enforcement officer transitioning from work life, where she or he frequently handles major issues using a reactive orientation, to her or his personal life, where the proactive demands required in making a decision to go to dinner can be an overwhelming task. It sounds like the paper or plastic dilemma in chapter 6. As difficult as it is to believe, "Surprise me" and "I don't know, whatever you want is okay with me" are not signs of active engagement in conversation or flexibility. They are signs of apathetic disengagement. This again is classic decision making (or lack thereof) at the bottom of the biological rollercoaster.

Self-perceived victim police officers who do not have an aggressive sense of time management would just wait and see what happens—they would "go with the flow." "Whatever you'd like, babe, is fine with me"; "Your call, honey, I'm down for anything you'd like to do." Survivors, on the other hand, would clearly understand that they need to develop a sense of control of their personal time and decision making. They would have been trained to develop the insight that when they return home from a shift of effective law enforcement and hypervigilance, the last thing they will want to do is make a decision. They have been trained to not wait until that point in time to make the decision. It's already been made and scheduled, and all the officer has to do is engage and do it.

With emotional survival and time-management training, police officers learn to appreciate the important need to take control of their personal lives and become proactive. They are trained to recognize the feeling of being drained, depleted, and exhausted after work as a symptom of hypervigilance, that swing from the sympathetic branch to the parasympathetic branch of the autonomic nervous system. More important, they are trained in how to overcome the feeling and not let it control their personal lives.

Schedule the Time

When I've interviewed police officers who have an orientation toward emotional survival, one of the fundamental characteristics these officers possess is a clearly controlled sense of personal time management and goal setting. Survivors realize that the last thing they want to do when they return home is make a decision, so they develop a strategy to make the decision at an earlier point in time. The officer, for example, has a goal of running three miles after work. The goal is written down. The officer knows what the after-work goal is and does it. The officer doesn't wait for the "feeling to go run three miles" to arrive. That feeling is never going to arrive while the officer is in the bottom of the rollercoaster. The officer just does it. The decision has already been made, and the officer knows what he or she is going to do, the goal has already been set. How do they develop this orientation? They have been trained in the basic skills of personal time management.

Ironically, victims might even know the skills and apply them in their professional lives, for example, when they are investigating a complex case that

Survivors realize that the last thing they want to do when they return home is make a decision, so they develop a strategy to make the decision at an earlier point in time.

requires managing several dimensions, but rarely do they utilize it in their personal lives. Survivors learn to be disciplined in their personal time orientation. They have personal life activities and goals in which they invest emotion off duty. This basically means they maintain a preplanned, written personal calendar or agenda that lists goals, requirements, and choices in their personal time that they will implement. By controlling personal time, officers take control of their personal lives. *Taking control* is a basic survivor orientation.

> *"I don't have control if the idiot chief requires that I wear a hat when I step out of the patrol car, but I do have control of coaching my daughter's softball team tonight."*

Although it sounds quite simplistic, a personal schedule is highly effective. It's self-empowering and increases emotional resiliency. The victim's orientation toward time is quite different from the survivor's. One law enforcement officer, a fifteen-year officer with a significant victim orientation, whom I interviewed about how he controls his personal time, gave a rather telling response:

> *"My personal life is not my responsibility. I just show up and it happens."*

Survivors would respond quite differently. They would realize that the hardest step on any journey is the first. They would realize, because of emotional survival training, that upon returning home, the last thing they would like to do is make a decision about what the evening's or day's activities will be. They wouldn't leave those decisions until the last minute, when they are realistically unlikely to make them. The concept of a preplanned, personal written calendar means that officers and families have become disciplined in terms of aggressively managing their personal time. They would take the time to put into writing activities they need or want to conduct over the course of the next week or two. They would begin developing an orientation of looking forward to specific things at specific times. The orientation of setting personal goals and seeing them fulfilled is self-empowering.

Victims very rarely experience this state. Their worldview is controlled by others. Survivors see themselves in charge of their personal agenda. Without specific time and goal-setting plans, the off-duty officer is basically like a person going to do the week's grocery shopping without a shopping list.

The victim officer looks forward to taking his or her children camping

"when things slow down at work"

"when it isn't so crazy at work"

"when I get a little more time on the job."

The survivor officer looks forward to taking his or her children camping

"two weekends from now"

"The 21st, 22nd, and 23rd of this month"

Which officer do you think actually takes the children camping, the vague victim or the specific survivor? The reality is that both officers probably equally love their children. It's just that aggressive time management permits one to demonstrate it through action.

These activities can be as mundane as cutting the grass or as necessary as taking the children to a dental appointment. Survivors control what is taking place in their personal lives and realize that they are not controlling most of the events taking place at the police agency. By controlling their personal time, they turn off police work and turn on a personal life. This increase in off-duty activities can also create the time and opportunity to continue doing many of the activities that could have become "I ustas." Survivor officers do not disengage from family activities and responsibilities.

Cops versus Firefighters

Is being a first responder the only reason for the reactive-dominated mode of time management by cops? Why do firefighters appear to be better able to harness off-duty time then cops? Well, if we poke a little friendly fun at the brother and sister first responders in the Fire Department, the answers might appear. Obviously, firefighters are the epitome of being reactive while in their professional on-duty mode. Why are they better able to be proactive in their off-duty world? Firefighters are absolutely reactive—the alarm goes off and they race to respond. They risk their lives, and they save the lives of others. The realities, however, are that the firefighter, even on duty, does not need to remain in the constant state of hypervigilance for the entire shift. The alarm is the starter's gun for the race to begin. An old adage states:

> *"You can be brain dead and be a firefighter—until there is a fire."*

The alarm starts the hypervigilance biological response for the firefighter. If there is no alarm sounding, the firefighter remains in the fire station in a fairly normal biological state. When the alarm sounds, the firefighters react biologically and respond as a group of trusted team members and provide their first responder services. The call for service is completed, and the firefighters return to the fire station as a group and stand down. They debrief and prepare their equipment for the next call for services. The alarm sounding for the firefighter starts the biological response of hypervigilance. Until the alarm sounds, there is no state of hypervigilance. The biological response for the firefighter returns to normal after the specific event is completed.

While firefighters experience hypervigilance during the call for service, cops experience hypervigilance the entire on-duty shift. Cops don't get an alarm. Cops *are* the alarm. Cops get a ? that they have to figure out. Hypervigilance is a state the firefighter moves into and out of depending on the number of calls for service on any given shift. The cop remains in hypervigilance for the entire duration of the shift. Cops have always poked friendly fun at firefighters because of the nature of their workload. Ask cops what firefighters do, and the often-heard reply is

> *"Sleep until you're hungry and eat until you're tired."*

The alarm bell initiates the biological response for firefighters, but the remaining time between calls for service permits firefighters to return to normal biology and normal social behavior. Firefighters eat meals as a group and go into dangerous situations as a group. They learn intense trust of their fellow firefighters. Cops go into dangerous situations often as individuals and learn distrust to stay alive. They learn this distrust, aka officer safety, and they practice it in a very heightened state of biological hypervigilance for the entire shift. Cops don't get an alarm.

Actually, the alarm itself has been problematic for firefighters. Many fire departments over the years have had to study how to tone out calls for service because the initial biological response to the alarm tone had initiated such intense biologically conditioned reactions from the firefighters. Some have experienced physical reactions such as tachycardia to the quick change in physiological states. Firefighters must put the pedal down and go from 0 to 100 in a few seconds. Cops remain at around 80 all shift and drop it to 100 when the situation requires. Hypervigilance is constant for the cop.

Not only does the situational versus constant state of hypervigilance create differences between the firefighter and the cop, but work schedules play a major role. Traditionally firefighters are deployed in some form of twenty-four-hour shift assignment. These extended shifts permit the firefighter to have large blocks of time off from work. The available blocks of free time from firefighter work demands make it easier to make the transition to personal life and to develop non-work-related competencies.

Police officers' work schedules are typically broken into smaller segments of each day. Traditionally cops worked eight-hour shift assignments, but ten- or twelve-hour shift assignments have become more the norm. Even with the extended number of work hours in a given day, cops must make the transition to off-duty life far more frequently over the average work week. Making the frequent transition to off duty without good time-management and goal-setting strategies undoes the personal life of many good cops. The longer work shifts of firefighters translates into nine or ten work shifts per month (or as cops would say, nine or ten sleepovers with BBQs per month). Cops oftentimes work fifteen to twenty shifts per month, not including overtime shifts. This requires the officer to develop skills of returning to their personal lives and learning how to engage and harness time management and goal setting.

Make the Time

One of the major difficulties in time orientation for police officers is that many think that they can't find the time to do what they want to do in their personal lives. They need to *make the time* to do what they want to do. Without emotional survival training, and with the development of a victim mindset, officers will find that the realities of police work and the magic chair will combine with the reactive professional orientation to fill each and every day between vigilance at work with the magic chair at home. The only thing that changes is the date.

A Personal Time-Management Calendar

Below is an example of a preplanned, written personal calendar. This calendar is a simple tool of time management that you and your family can use. Although many officers keep calendars on a digital device, often it's best to post a hard copy in any area shared by the entire family. Many police officers and families put their calendar on the refrigerator, where it becomes a central focal point for activities and decisions that affect them.

Weekly Calendar

S	M	T	W	Th	F	Sa

If a police officer and family have developed the orientation of proactive time control, making the decision to go out to dinner might look entirely different than it does in the "Are You a Reactive Decision Maker?" box earlier in this chapter. Instead of the "wait until Friday night" strategy, the police couple might have discussed the decision several days earlier and placed it on their calendar. The couple's conversation might look different.

Officer: What do you think if this Friday we go out to grab a bite to eat after work, just to celebrate the weekend?

Significant other: That sounds pretty good. Where do you want to go?

Officer: Let's go on down and grab a steak at that new restaurant.

Significant other: Sounds good. I'll give Pete and Sally a call and see if they want to join us.

The couple then sticks it on their calendar and has something to look forward to that *they control.* If you ask officers about this inter-action—what has the officer just done when committing, in writing, to activities in his or her personal life?—many officers will respond:

"The officer has taken control and has something to look forward to."

Many of the more cynical victim-oriented officers, however, when asked what the officer has done by putting things in writing, will respond:

"They've taken a major step toward disappointment."

"I don't make plans. Every time you plan something, the department will screw you out of it"

"That's just total bullshit. Soon as you make plans to do something, you know one of those asshole com-manders is going to have you work overtime, or you'll

get called out. It's a hell of a lot easier just to not make plans. Then you won't get screwed out of them by the department."

"You take vacation around here, that's when they're going to transfer you or screw with you for sure."

"I'm saving my vacation time so that if they screw with me, I'll have some time on the books to take care of business."

Listening to the cynical officers, the victim theme comes through loud and clear. Their whole orientation toward time is from a victim perspective. This doesn't mean these victim officers didn't learn that orientation from reality; in fact, they probably did get screwed out of plans and activities many times over the course of their police careers. However, these officers need to honestly answer this question:

"How often does the agency actually screw you out of your plans?"

Victim officers will respond, "All the time. Every time I make plans, they screw me over." Survivors, on the other hand, might assume a more quantitatively accurate perspective and say, "Oh, 20 or 30 percent of the time they screw up my plans." Survivors will put a number to how many times their personal lives have been invaded by the professional demands of the job. Clearly, the realities are that the personal life of the law enforcement officer will be invaded by the demands of the law enforcement career. Remember my perspective on this issue. "No one escapes their police career with their professional virginity intact. Everyone gets screwed by the agency at least one time."

The difficulty is that victims, early in their careers, can combine the immediate sense of disappointment from having personal plans arbitrarily canceled because of agency needs with the vegetative-like state of the magic chair and cease to aggressively and proactively control their personal lives. Instead of recognizing, as survivors do, that 70 to 80 percent of the time, their plans are *not* canceled, they take a victim orientation toward their personal time and the days become weeks, and weeks become months, with little other than work being accomplished.

This loss of time-management skills can occur early in a police career. While I was conducting a training session in "Emotional Survival," a young officer took exception to the concept of needing to learn good personal time-management skills. The following is the exchange:

Young officer: This is ridiculous. Every time you plan something, you'll get screwed out of it. I quit making plans for my personal life when I became a cop.

Author: Every time they've been canceled. Gosh, well what's the next thing you're looking forward to?

Young officer: Retirement

Author: Well, I can tell you from personal experience that retirement from police work is great, but you're twenty-six.

How many times does the perception of time in a cop's life deteriorate to two timeframes? The first timeframe is when cops tells you what they "usta do" before they became cops. The second timeframe, after maybe a decade on the job, is when they begin telling you what they are "going to do" once they retire. Listening to cops talk about past activities they previously engaged in and the wistful longing for the freedom to do the things they are going to do at some distant retirement time only points out the need for time-management skills here and now. Remember the previous case history of the narcotics officer in chapter 6, reflecting on his lack of involvement in his children's lives? Would that very dedicated police officer, who would have laid his life down for his children, still view his role as father as inadequate if he had been able to harness time each day of his children's developmental years?

If an officer goes to work, comes home each day, and rides the magic chair for the remainder of his or her personal life, it sets up an interesting mathematical computation: Let's say the officer does nothing in his or her personal life each day for a thousand days. If you multiply nothing times a thousand, what do you get?

Nothing!

One of the basic reasons that the personal lives of many police officers are lost is due not to a conscious effort to cease engaging in off-duty activities, but rather to a loss of a sense of control of the time to do the activities, compounded by postwork parasympathetic exhaustion.

The frequency of non-work-related activity diminishes over the first few years of police work until it basically no longer exists. Learning to aggressively control personal time is a fundamental element of becoming an emotional survivor. Officers develop an orientation from which they clearly appreciate that there is an amount of time each day that the agency controls, but that there's also a significant amount of time each day that they control—the time in their personal lives. The rollercoaster causes the victim officers to abdicate all control of the very manner in which they view their daily personal time. This loss of control clearly facilitates the development of a victim orientation. Beliefs such as "There's never enough time" become the daily orientation of many law enforcement officers. Putting personal time control back in the hands of officers begins with truly understanding the concept of *personal empowerment.*

Time Management and Relationships

Survivors are empowered people. They know that they run each day in their lives, and they actually go forth and run it. Victims have a sense of having been wronged and focus on retribution or retaliation against those they see as the party that victimized them, typically the agency where they are employed. Survivors have a different orientation toward priorities in life. Although many law enforcement officers would profess that they love their husband, wife, or children, it would be interesting to see how much time they invest each day in the people they profess to love. Unfortunately, children and domestic partners can become secondary in the life of a law enforcement officer who is oscillating between the two pendulous extremes of the biological rollercoaster.

One law enforcement officer, a fourteen-year veteran, discussed his loss of personal time control and how it affected his marriage:

> *"My wife told me that she knew she was the most important thing in my life. She just wanted to know if she was the most important thing in my day."*

The officer went on to relate that his wife's question caused him to significantly reassess his priorities each day. He stated that it was very difficult to spend the entire day highly energized and vigilant, "putting fires out" as a police officer, then return home and give his personal life and the people he loved the attention they deserved and that he wanted to give them. He didn't know how to do it.

The Greatest Accomplishment

An officer who understood the importance of aggressive time management was asked during his retirement dinner by the chief of police, "Looking back on your career, what do you think your greatest accomplishment as a police officer was these last twenty years?"

The officer stated firmly, "I didn't miss one of my three children's basketball games over the years that each of them were in high school."

The chief thought this was a rather unique response and asked him to elaborate. The officer went on, "For me to make each of my three sons' basketball games required more work and proactive scheduling than handling any case or investigation that I had as a police officer. I had to change days off, reschedule off-duty work details, and even beg prosecutors to use me at a different point in their trial. It took a significant effort. As I look back, I have more pride in the fact that I didn't miss even one of my sons' basketball games than any sense of accomplishment in all the idiots I wrote tickets to or arrested."

In many ways this officer is highly justified in his sense of accomplishment and pride in not having missed one of his sons' basketball games. Over the course of his lifetime, his proactive effort and management of his personal time reaped significantly more dividends for his overall emotional survival than a few more hours riding the hypervigilance rollercoaster—sitting at home watching television, surfing the internet, or working some off-duty employment detail—ever would have.

The fundamental core issue for survivor law enforcement officers is to possess a belief that they run their personal lives. They are in control of their personal lives, and they invest significant emotional energy and time in that part of their lives. This is a basic separation in orientation between the victim and the survivor. The victim begins viewing life and personal time as something to be endured until "retirement and I can get away from these assholes and start living my own life." The survivor, on the other hand, has a sense of mastery, empowerment, and control of his or her day-to-day life in the here and now. Part of the law enforcement culture is an almost obsessive discussion of retirement, many times by people in their thirties.

"When I retire, it's KMA time. I'm going to play golf five days a week."

"When I retire, we'll be down in Florida before the ink dries on my paperwork" (for East Coast cops)

"I'll be out of here so fast—we got a place in Idaho" (for West Coast cops)

This retirement discussion many years before retirement in reality is not an example of good planning ahead. It is a desire and longing for a time that permits a feeling of self-autonomy and self-determination. It's a desire to be free from being in a position of emotional subservience to the people who control the work role. By not having good time management skills and learning to invest emotionally in their personal lives, ironically and tragically overinvested officers actually further enhance the feeling of subservience. The more they overinvest in the police role, the more powerful they make the people who control that role. The victim continues to invest emotional energy into those they feel have victimized them. People with an aggressive sense of running their own personal lives do not waste time ruminating or obsessing over perceived wrongs by the agency. Rather, they aggressively attempt to live life to the fullest by overcoming the deleterious effects of the biological rollercoaster and the magic chair. They live *today*, not in some far-off time and wishful place called "retirement."

Case History

Once on a multiple-day fishing trip to a renowned steelhead river in the Pacific Northwest with five cops, I experienced a young officer's lack of living in the here and now. Because of the size of the river and the volume of current flow, for safety, the group was divided in pairs so that no one would need to wade the river alone. For three days I fished with a young cop who constantly kept "bitching" about what an asshole his chief was. On the final day, this young officer had worn out my patience, and the following exchange occurred.

Author: I don't think your chief is an asshole.

Young cop: You don't have to work for him.

Author: You're right, I don't have to work for him, but you know what, I know a few hundred chiefs of police, and you know one. Let me tell you something. On the continuum of assholeishness, your chief is just not that big an asshole. But I'll stipulate that you're right,

continued

your chief is an asshole, but let me ask a you a question: Was he an asshole yesterday?

Young cop: He's been an asshole for the four years I've known him.

Author: Do you think he's still an asshole today?

Young cop: That's a stupid question. Of course he's still an asshole today. Where are you going with these stupid questions?

Author: Well now, I was just thinking, if you've known him for four years, and he's been an asshole the whole time, and you say he was an asshole yesterday, and you're 100 percent certain he is still an asshole today, I think you can just relax and assume he will still be an asshole tomorrow when we get off the river. So why don't you quit talking about this guy. I'm tired of hearing about this guy. He's a hundred miles from here, and I'm pretty sure he isn't thinking about you. Let's just catch these fish, drink some beers, eat those steaks they're cooking back at camp, and enjoy life. Quit letting crazy shit live in your head rent-free

I'm not sure if the young cop learned anything from our exchange. I did learn, however, why the other older cops in our group pawned him off to me as a fishing partner. Personally, I felt sad to watch a fine young officer become trapped in the world of emotional overinvestment and feeling like a victim. In a beautiful outdoor setting, with the fish biting and the beer cold, this young officer continued to invest emotional energy only into the cop role, which the chief controlled. The older survivor cops had dragged him along on the trip. Hopefully, their intervention might initiate some time management and goal setting in the young cop, and he'll get himself back on the water and feeling more personally empowered.

Many young police officers talk about how over the course of the first few years in the force, their marriages and relationships change and are redefined. Marriages often end because, from the involved parties' perspective, "We fell out of love with each other." Although on occasion that clearly does happen, how often do marriages end because there is a significant lack of time spent together in joint efforts and activities? That joint activity could be working to achieve some shared goals or just sharing fun with each other during recreational pursuits. Many law enforcement relationships die on the vine because the officer is so caught up in the rollercoaster ride, he or she fails to cultivate the relationship. Relationships that once were dynamic and loving can be destroyed by lack of emotional investment and energy. Loving someone with your heart alone is not enough to pass through the years together—you have to love someone also with your time.

Case History

While waiting to begin instructing a class on "Emotional Survival" to a large auditorium of law enforcement folks, I was approached by an officer carrying multiple copies of the first edition of this book. An interesting conversation ensued:

Officer: Good morning Dr. Gilmartin, can I ask you for a favor? Would you please sign my books?

Author: I'd be honored to. Who can I address the books to?

Officer: My ex-wives.

Author: Ex-wives as in plural?

Officer: Yeah, I have three of them. I refer to them as P-1, P-2, and P-3 for Plaintiff -1, Plaintiff-2, and Plaintiff-3 because they are always suing me.

Author: You better be careful that they don't get a class action suit against you. [I was thinking that the officer was just making a joke, but it soon became obvious that he was not joking.] You're serious. You want me to address books to your ex-wives?   continued

Officer: Yes, please.

Author: I've never been asked to address books to an officer's former spouse or spouses. Can I ask why you want me to address the books to your former spouses?

Officer: I just want to say that I'm sorry for what happened to our marriages and wish them the best in the future. The divorces were 100 percent my fault, and I want them to understand, it wasn't anything they caused. I just want to give some closure to them.

Author: [At this point I was very concerned about the officer possibly being self-destructive and wanting to get closure on past emotional issues. After signing three books, a fourth book remained.] There's a fourth book: Who should I make that out to?

Officer: Oh, that's for my wife. She's here with me today.

Author: So you have number 4 with you today?

Officer: No, Doc, I have number 1 with me here today. This is actually my first marriage where I'm an active partner. After my last divorce, I was really down. I knew I needed to talk to someone. I went to the Employee's Assistance Program, and they put me in a support group with other cops, and we had to read a bunch of books, including this one. Talking with the other cops and discussing all those different books, I realized that I was blessed. I had three good women come into my life and agree to share their life with me and be my life partner. I had three families, and I screwed it up three times, and I hurt a lot of people because of that. I just want to tell them that I'm sorry. They didn't cause the divorces, I did, but I had no idea what was going on in my life. I don't live like that anymore. This marriage now is Until Death Do Us Part. I'm an active member of this relationship. I just want my ex-wives to understand what happened and wish them the best in their future.

> They're good people and the mothers of my children. Doc, I learned this stuff the hard way. Why can't we teach it to the young cops, so they don't have to learn it the hard way? Why can't we speed up the learning curve?

Survivors Practice Physical Fitness

The second major element of the survival orientation is an awareness, obtained through training, that the hypervigilance biological rollercoaster® is physiological in nature. Therefore, any remedy will also need to be in part physiological. Ironically, this insight was also obtained in the police retirees' interviews. When asked about regrets, as mentioned above, the first regret dealt with wishing they had spent more time with their children when the kids had been young. The second most frequent regret:

"I wished I had stayed in better shape after the academy."

Considering how much time, effort, and expense is invested in physical fitness during the recruit-training phase in law enforcement, it is bewildering how it is almost immediately ignored in many law enforcement agencies upon graduation from the academy. Almost all the energy invested during training for recruits is focused on being physically able to handle the demands of the career. Defensive tactics, mobility, dynamic strength, and reaction time are all very accurately seen as benefiting from physical fitness. The emotional and stress-reduction benefits of physical fitness are almost totally ignored.

The bottom half of the biological rollercoaster plunges officers into the parasympathetic branch. The traits of the parasympathetic branch mimic depression: apathetic, isolated, tired, detached, disengaged. Ironically, studies have demonstrated that as little as twenty minutes per day of walking briskly on a treadmill produces results with clinically depressed patients identical to the results of treatment with antidepressant medication. Over recent decades, as the movement to provide employee assistance and mental health services to law enforcement personnel has increased, tragically physical fitness has all but been left out of the discussion.

The pendulous swing between the highs and lows of the roller-coaster are the body's way of attempting to recalibrate or balance the effects of the extreme physical reactions caused by hypervigilance. This need to balance, or find homeostasis biologically, is a necessary process, and it can be facilitated by even moderate physical fitness. Although hypervigilance is a necessary worldview if law enforcement officers are to survive a career that exposes them to potential risk each day, officers do have the option of not passively waiting at the bottom half of the rollercoaster for the effects to correct themselves. Physical fitness will accelerate movement out of the lower reaches of the rollercoaster and back into the normal range of emotion. Physical fitness moves the off-duty officer upward, back between the lines and into the normal range of emotion and social interaction.

Obviously, physical fitness has benefits for a law enforcement officer far beyond breaking the emotional effect of the rollercoaster. In terms of muscular flexibility and the possession of the necessary dynamic strength to perform job duties, physical fitness is fundamental for the officer's physical survival. The extreme paradox of the hypervigilance cycle is that it keeps cops alive in the short term, but in reality it brings the potential for elevated premature death rates for police officers in the long run.

To understand the extreme long-term deleterious physical effects of hypervigilance requires fully understanding a few specific biological dynamics of the rollercoaster. When officers go on duty and enter the elevated phase of the hypervigilance cycle for survival, the *adrenal-cortical* stress reaction of the sympathetic branch is being engaged. Adrenaline (cortisol) begins to flow. Cortisol has multiple functions, but it primarily regulates the body's metabolism. It also helps regulate blood pressure and blood glucose levels, reduce inflammation, and affect memory functioning.

As hypervigilance causes the initiation of the adrenal-cortical stress response, cortisol triggers the liver to release blood glucose into the bloodstream. The elevated blood glucose is to be used as the source of energy to face the threat that is taking place. Hypervigilance for officer safety basically means the officer is in an elevated state of potential threat perception all shift. It also basically means that the adrenal-cortical stress response is taking place the entire shift. The elevated blood glucose released from the liver is the physiological basis of the subjective feelings experienced at the top of the biological rollercoaster—alive, energized, and quick thinking. This elevated engaged state is necessary for officer safety. It is the short-term response for survival but the long-term beginning of disease process.

As the cortisol-released blood glucose flows into the bloodstream, the pancreas releases insulin. This insulin captures a significant amount of the blood glucose and infuses it into fat cells to be stored in reserve to address the pending threat. It is basically the biological equivalent of carrying an extra magazine for your weapon to have resources kept in reserve. Insulin is the fat storage hormone. The glucose is infused into the fat cells, particularly the abdominal area fat cells, for ready availability for metabolism to address the threat. This biological reaction to stress in most people is a fairly infrequent occurrence. In police officers, it is a daily occurrence and becomes inseparable from the police role. It is the biological foundation of the rollercoaster. So when older cops have said "this type of work gets into your blood," they were physiologically correct.

Unfortunately, the adrenal-cortical stress reaction is not meant to be a daily occurrence. The pendulous swing of the stages of the biological rollercoaster triggering elevated glucose daily becomes problematic for several reasons. First, the daily constant infusion of glucose into the abdominal lipid (fat) cells causes cops to get fat. Incremental weight gain has become, unfortunately, almost accepted in police culture. Some studies have found that over 40 percent of police officers are clinically obese. The daily constant experience of hypervigilance and constant glucose infusion by law enforcement officers versus the only episodic infusion by firefighters is why women buy calendars of minimally clad firefighters and don't buy calendars of cops with their shirts off. No one wants to see a calendar of cops with their shirts off. What would you call that calendar? *Badges and Bellies?*

This incremental weight gain is nature's way of preserving the entity when facing threat and is no different from what other mammals experience. Every autumn, bears, for example, must prepare to survive the threat of the coming winter. There will be no food for the bear to forage during the winter months, so without intervention, it will starve to death. Every autumn, with the threat of coming winter, the bear's adrenal-cortical stress response surges. The bear's liver releases glucose into the bloodstream. This elevated glucose energizes the bear to go on foraging rampages, and the bear consumes large amounts of food and gets fat in preparation for the coming winter. The reality, however, is that a bear will double its body fat content during the month of October even if all food is withheld from the bear. It doesn't get fat solely because it eats a lot. The bear gets fat because, thanks to cortisol, it stores a lot. It enters this stage of adrenal-cortical stress response in preparation for hibernation once a year. The cop enters the stage of adrenal-cortical stress response once a shift for the entire shift. Firefighters enter the response only while working specific calls. That's why they're on the calendars and the cops aren't.

Although the stereotype of the fat cop and the relationship between cops and doughnuts has been the brunt of jokes for a long time, it is not a joking matter. Incremental weight gain in cops signals the movement toward a specific disease process. The cop is moving toward *metabolic syndrome.* The daily infusion of glucose into the fat cells, across the cell wall and through the cellular glucose receptor, breaks down over time. Glucose secreted by the stress reaction is no longer infused into the fat cell and remains in the bloodstream. The blood glucose level begins its slow march toward disease. Unfortunately, the standard medical assessment of blood glucose uses a measurement, A1C, that is basically too little and too late. By the time the standard measurement reaches pathological levels, the officer is already borderline diabetic or has become type II diabetic.

This biological march toward a disease with potentially life-ending consequences appears all but totally ignored in the average law enforcement agency. The increased death rates of heart disease and stroke due to this disease progression can be several hundred percent higher than the predisease risk factors suggest. Addressing incremental weight gain in police is a necessity, not for physical appearance purposes but to derail a disease process brought on by the daily adrenal-cortical stress response of hypervigilance.

Genetic factors also clearly play a role in some percentage of this disease process. Certain ethnic and racial groups are at statistically far greater risk. Unfortunately, these risks are almost totally ignored over the course of law enforcement officers' work years, but they significantly shorten their life in the retirement years. Remember those "retirement years" when the officers were going to "play golf five days a week"? Unfortunately for far too many cops, those years either don't take place or are significantly shortened.

Physical fitness is not a luxury for law enforcement officers; it's a basic requirement if they are to become emotional survivors.

The intervention to derail this disease process is so simple it is almost criminal that it is ignored in police organizations. The U.S. Centers for Disease Control and Prevention (CDC) relates that losing 5 to 7 percent of body weight—that's 10 to 14 pounds for a 200-pound person—and getting at least 150 minutes of moderate physical activity each week reduces the risk of type 2 diabetes by nearly 60 percent in those at high risk and nearly 70 percent in average risk groups for developing the disease. Getting 150 minutes of moderate exercise per week means 21.5 minutes per day. Be extravagant and round it off to 22 minutes per day. This amount of moderate exercise to reduce the disease that is the major lifetime killer of cops by between 60 and 70 percent seems like an extremely small investment in time and expense. The dividends are lifesaving.

Physical fitness is not a luxury for law enforcement officers; it's a basic requirement if they are to become emotional survivors.

Time in the gym is as critical for mental wellness and resiliency for law enforcement as is the provision of competent professional counseling services. It also needs to be seen as a basic requirement to maintain a professional workforce that can perform their duties effectively and ethically in highly emotionally charged situations. Cops need to make split-second decisions, often after intense physical exertion. The 35-pound-overweight officer with an elevated resting pulse cannot be expected to perform in those situations. It's both a health time bomb and an operational performance nightmare waiting to detonate.

Therefore, officers who are physical and emotional survivors live their personal lives not in the depressive-like ranges at the bottom of the rollercoaster but rather between the lines. They're spontaneous, outgoing, and engaged in personal activities. They have moved out of the depressive off-duty phase, and their personal lives reap the benefits. They also have the physical attributes to perform in the very intense situations that require immediate action and decision making. Their lives, the lives of fellow cops, and the lives of members of the public depend on physically fit police officers. It is tragic that the police profession has languished far behind the fire service in appreciating this practice.

What Kind of Exercise?
Moving up from the bottom of the rollercoaster back within the normal range can be accomplished by very moderate aerobic exercise. The CDC recommendation of 150 minutes per week, or 22 minutes per day, can be a guideline and a starting point to address the psychological issues. Obviously, however, the job of police officer also requires dynamic strength and conditioning with specific skills to address operational demands and performance. For police officers to defend themselves during assaults or make life and death decisions in shoot/don't shoot situations demands physical fitness. The law enforcement profession looking at this concept like an ostrich with its head in the sand has cost far too many lives—lives lost to either operational failure or situational depression that physical competency and fitness could have prevented.

The Effect of Exercise on the
Biological Rollercoaster

On Duty

Alive, Alert, Energetic, Involved, Humorous

Tired, Detached, Isolated, Apathetic

Off Duty

In the figure above, notice that the arrow has moved from the bottom of the rollercoaster back to the normal range. The impact of exercise on the hypervigilance rollercoaster is one of the paradoxes of the physiological effects of hypervigilance. If you were physically exhausted from the expenditure of muscular energy doing manual labor and then returned to your personal life and physically exercised, this exercise would only further enhance your sense of exhaustion. The detachment, isolation, fatigue, and apathy that typify the bottom reaches of the hypervigilance rollercoaster for police, however, respond positively to physical exercise. It is mood elevating. Ask any group of law enforcement officers how they feel after they exercise, and they inevitably respond: "Tired, but a lot better." Physical exercise not only raises the behavioral activity level of the officer, but it also has significant stress-reducing components that give the officer a sense of relaxation and generalized well-being.

Moderate physical exercise is also an essential element in any program of anger reduction. Chronically angry cops don't make good decisions. The physiological consequence of hypervigilance leaves law enforcement officers feeling detached, isolated, and apathetic to social interaction; however, it can also leave them with a sense of irritability, frustration, and emotional volatility. One of the tragedies facing law enforcement families is officers returning home after dealing with unsolvable social problems only to have the frustration, irritability, and anger caused by the job transferred into domestic violence after experiencing a normal disagreement or annoyance at home. Officers who are angry often transfer that emotional distress into physically inappropriate behavior. Officers and families say things they can't take back, and unfortunately, this can lead to acts of physical violence. Not only is moderate physical fitness a key element in breaking the destructive aspects of the biological rollercoaster, but it also provides officers a much-needed physical outlet and relief valve to drain the effects of generalized job stress, as well as helping maintain an overall wellness-based lifestyle.

The insight the officer and family obtain through training in emotional survival shows them how terribly important a continuing physical fitness and exercise program can be. Many police officers will discuss physical fitness after ten years as officers and say, "I usta be very fit. I ran every day. I usta go to the gym." The "I usta" syndrome plays a major role in the disappearance or reduction of physical fitness in the lives of law enforcement officers.

A few law enforcement agencies in recent years have begun stressing on-duty physical fitness and providing workout areas or exercise rooms for personnel. Unfortunately, no small number of these agencies have invested their monetary resources into strength-related equipment only, which, although highly beneficial for the health and strength of the officer, do not have as direct an effect on the hypervigilance rollercoaster as do aerobic exercise regimens. Aerobic exercise is any exercise that is rhythmic and repetitive and places the emphasis on the exchange of oxygen and carbon dioxide. It focuses on the cardiovascular system and places the target heart rate as a goal of exercise. Some agencies have invested in structured peer-driven cross-training-type programs that incorporate the full range of fitness demands required of police officers. These appear most effective.

Resistance to Exercise

Law enforcement officers typically begin their careers highly knowledgeable and sophisticated in terms of physical fitness—the academies see to that. As the years pass and the biological rollercoaster takes its toll, however, officers stop applying their knowledge of physical fitness and begin living a sedentary off-duty lifestyle, which typifies too many law enforcement officers' day-to-day existence. Most officers do not need to be convinced of the benefits of exercise. They know the effects of exercise from previous stages in their lives. They *do* need help in making the exercise happen. They need to be made aware through emotional survival training of the necessity of physical fitness across their career and lifespans as a means of providing significant emotional assistance. Any intervention by an agency that helps its personnel develop programs of physical fitness plays a major role in the overall survival of its officers.

Unfortunately, the movement toward on-duty mandatory physical fitness training has become a point of conflict between labor and management across the

> *The very act of engaging in physical fitness means officers are taking control of and responsibility for their time and actions each day.*

profession. It is not uncommon to find individual law enforcement officers who are resistant to physical fitness. It's even more unfortunate to find either a labor union or management team that has been organizationally hijacked by a victim culture and uses the fitness program as a point of leverage conflict. Some individual officers are aggressively resistant to the idea of physical fitness and even internalize it into their worldview. It's not uncommon to hear officers say:

"If they want me to jog, how come they give me a patrol car?"

"If they're going to make me exercise, they're going to pay me while I'm doing it."

It's interesting how many officers, even when their agency allots a set number of hours per month for physical fitness, still resist the concept of aggressively taking a sense of responsibility for and control of their day-to-day physical activity. One of the significant benefits of a maintained and disciplined physical fitness program is that it sets a time each day during which officers put the demands of police work on the back burner and take responsibility for and control of their own behavior. They are performing the core elements of being a survivor: controlling their own lives. A sustained physical fitness program will rarely be found in the day-to-day life of many cops who view the world as a victim.

The victim officer will say, "I know I need to exercise, but I just can't find the time." The individual who sets aside time each day to take responsibility for his or her 22 minutes of physical fitness will also take responsibility for other personal life aspects that previously had been put on the back burner or abandoned. The very act of engaging in physical fitness means officers are taking control of and responsibility for their time and actions each day. It's a simple concept of personal responsibility that changes lives and is easy to remember:

Do 22

Cops and Sleep

Surviving police work both emotionally and physically requires that the officer be trained in sleep hygiene. But maintaining healthy sleep regimens is a rare topic of discussion in law enforcement training either at the recruit or in-service levels. Although sleep researchers agree that people need an absolute minimum of seven hours and preferably eight hours of good-quality sleep daily, more than 80 percent of police officers report inadequate sleep.

This sleep deficit is a major contributing factor to emotional and behavioral issues with police officers. Some sleep researchers have found that nearly half the police officers studied required referral to a physician for intervention because sleep impairment had reached clinically diagnosable levels.

The Classic Symptoms of Sleep Deficiency

- decreased alertness
- impaired reaction time and task performance
- loss of impulse control
- interference with decision making
- loss of anger modulation
- exaggerated startle reaction

Sleep deficiency can lead to disastrous police behavior. Considering that among all professions, police officers are most frequently required to make split-second life-or-death decisions, sleep hygiene should be a high priority. Very few other professions require employees to make life-impacting decisions in a fraction of a second, in a dimly lighted setting, while out of breath from running after a suspect for a few hundred yards at 3:00 a.m.

The lack of training in sleep hygiene leaves many officers unaware of how chronic sleep shortage affects their lives. When speaking of sleep hygiene with officers, I often hear a common statement: "I go to sleep when I feel tired." That oversimplified response is fine, but what happens if the officer stops ever feeling tired? Years of disrupted sleep, changing work schedules, lengthy work-home travel commutes all combine to influence a large percentage of officers into taking a victim-like mindset when it comes to sleep management: "All those job-related intrusions are out of my control." Those officers are probably correct—those intrusion factors are out of their control—but creating a strategy to overcome the impact of the intrusions is not out of their control. Considering all the sleep intrusion factors affecting police officers, it is probably the most difficult area in which to develop a survivor-based *do-control* orientation. Nonetheless, it must be accomplished.

Teaching cops a few basic concepts of good sleep hygiene can prevent poor sleep habits from becoming transferred into tragic on-duty actions. Many astronaut candidates wash out of NASA's selection process because they cannot maintain uninterrupted sleep for the designated test period. The candidates wash out of the program because the demands of space travel cannot tolerate a suboptimal decision taking place. Suboptimal decisions by police officers often lead to tragedy and the criminal prosecution of good officers.

Attempting to take control of sleep hygiene requires officers to realize that they might not feel fatigue or sleepy at the time they need to retire for the day. Seven, preferably eight, hours of sleep being required puts the task on the officer to ensure "lights out" seven to eight hours before the time to awaken. This is very hard to do with the realities of a police officer's life. Every effort needs to be taken to accomplish the goal whenever possible.

To the extent possible, police families need to adjust schedules and living arrangements to facilitate healthy sleep environments at home. Bedrooms need to be transitioned into sleep-inducing settings. Keeping the bedroom as dark as possible might require the installation of total blackout curtains. Electronic entertainment devices should be removed from the sleeping environment. This means removing not only television sets from the bedroom, but also smart phones, tablets, and computers. The idea of checking your email or social media in bed before turning lights out might sound innocent enough, but the light spectrum of the cellphone has just affected the visual functioning of the brain, and now you're awake. If a cellphone is kept in the bedroom for alarm or security concerns, put it under a light-blocking cover. Even the charging indicator light is enough light to impact the hypervigilant brain. Officers comment on how much better they sleep in total darkness, as on a tent camping trip: "I'll be sleepy not long after it gets dark, and I'm up at the break of dawn." Light plays havoc on the cortisol levels of the brain, affecting sleep.

Bedrooms also need to be kept at a temperature cooler than what is normally used in the remainder of the home. Further, be aware of the impact of caffeine and alcohol on sleep. Adjust mealtimes so that you have adequate time after eating before you attempt to sleep. Also leave adequate time after physical exercise.

Exercise facilitates better sleeping hygiene overall, but it awakens the brain. When attempting to sleep, the goal is to slow down the brain. Many officers will say, "I just can't shut my brain off. I'll doze while watching TV in my chair, but when I head into the bedroom, I'm fully awake, and stuff starts popping into my head." When that happens, take a few minutes and jot down a note on what it is that you believe you need to be thinking about. Put the note aside and use it as an offshoot of a time-management technique. You don't need to think about it right now. It will be there to think about when you awaken and read your note.

Whenever possible, and this is hard to do in the real world of police work, attempt to retire at the same time each day. Setting good sleep habits is essential. Note that sleep disruption can also be caused by underlying medical conditions. If sleep disruption appears to be out of your control, seek medical attention and have it addressed. Tired cops are dangerous cops, to themselves and others. Make a commitment to yourself and your loved ones to not be working when pathologically tired. As mentioned in early chapters of this book, after twenty-four hours of sustained wakefulness, a police officer's reaction time and judgment is identical to that of someone with a blood alcohol equivalent of .10. Eighteen hours of sustained wakefulness is equivalent to .08 BAL. Please never go to work as a .08 or higher. The decisions police officers make are far too important.

Survivors Control Their Financial Well-Being

One surprising aspect of physical fitness and good sleep hygiene appears to be that officers who aggressively practice physical fitness and pursue physical activities in their personal lives appear to be somewhat more stable financially. The answer to this might lie in some simple behavioral observations. When marketing professionals observe consumer behavior, they note some significant gender differences in spending behavior. Speaking of gender differences at the present time can be like touching the third rail in terms of shouts of sexism, but it does need to be discussed in this aspect of developing a survivor orientation. The behavioral and marketing researchers on Madison Avenue have known this gender-based observation to be true for many years, and it drives gender-targeted advertising programs. They have clearly established that certain individuals, when feeling mildly depressed or unfocused, can find themselves feeling more energetic if they purchase something, and this form of mood-elevating "retail therapy" has distinct gender differences. Research indicates that women trend toward being more cautious financially and tend to make small ticket purchases, things that can be absorbed within the next budget cycle. Small items achieve the desired emotional response of "feeling better, feeling more alive." This traditionally female-gender approach to making purchases is more conservative and rarely involves a major purchase. Small purchases get the job done in terms of mood elevation. Many times the social component of "going shopping" after work and stopping for a glass of wine afterward with friends meets many emotional and social needs.

The traditionally male counterpart to this behavior, however, does not appear to be as simple nor as conservative. Men do not appear to like to "go shopping," but they do enjoy "buying stuff." What kinds of stuff do they enjoy buying? The men's stuff appears to be big-ticket items, aka "boys' toys"—boats, cars, pickup trucks, motor homes, campers, motorcycles, and maybe some power tools. The typical law enforcement spending pattern, for both male and female officers, unfortunately, appears to be more closely linked to the traditional male spending pattern. The items officers tend to purchase are large, and they are typically not absorbed within the next budget cycle. It does feel good to make the purchase, however:

> *"Why don't you come over and check out my new pickup truck? Man, I tell you what, this truck is just great. It has the new diesel engine and 4 x 4 transmission. I just love driving this truck. It's got the all-leather-interior package. It's a great truck. Man, I just love driving around in it."*

How long does this "great" feeling last? Until the first payment! How long do the payments last? Four or five years. How are those payments going to be made considering this purchase is not easily absorbed within the routine family budget cycle? The answer, again, is quite clear:

Work a few extra off-duty jobs or grab as much overtime as possible to make the payments.

This spending pattern can represent a vicious cycle that affects many officers and families who have not been trained in emotional survival. These families often fall prey to *stress-related consumerism.*

The Stress-Related Consumerism Cycle

Stress-related consumerism is an officer's attempt to move from the bottom reaches of the biological rollercoaster to the top by making novelty purchases. The cycle can become quite overwhelming for some officers who purchase a new vehicle or recreational toy and find themselves working every available off-duty job or taking all the available overtime to meet the financial obligations of the purchase. The cycle can become quite consuming. The officer's financial life can become one continuous interaction between making a major purchase that is designed to alleviate some psychological distress and provide some recreational panacea and the need to be forever increasing the number of off-duty jobs and overtime hours to address the new financial obligation. A vicious financial and off-duty work-related cycle has begun.

This cycle robs the officer of any sense of financial security across the span of the occupational career. Many officers, without having a sense of proactive control of their finances, experience significant distress economically, despite enjoying an occupational career that is generally free of layoffs and downsizing, with excellent retirement and medical benefits. Many officers have a lack of financial sophistication in reviewing their economic status. Living the rollercoaster across a career can produce a middle-aged law enforcement officer whose level of knowledge and awareness economically is not significantly greater than what typified the beginning of the career ten or fifteen years earlier. Quite frequently, the financial security of the law enforcement retirement program is a major factor in why a significant number of individuals remain in the law enforcement field long after the attractiveness or novelty of the job has passed. Ironically, the desire to obtain financial security in many officers is often limited to valuing only the retirement itself. Many law enforcement agencies provide excellent financial benefit packages, including deferred compensation programs, but often do not take adequate time to inform and educate their employees on the potential financial benefits available.

Financial frustration at an individual level can be transferred into collective-bargaining-unit frustrations with the management of an organization. Financial difficulties, as seen by an officer lacking in a sophisticated awareness of his or her financial status, on more than one occasion have led to inappropriate ethical and even criminal violations of trust relationships when an officer takes inappropriate actions, motivated by short-term financial gain. Providing law enforcement officers with a sophisticated awareness of the potential financial benefit packages available, as is done in the private sector, would create an increased sense of financial security as officers approach the latter years of their law enforcement careers. A sense of appreciation of financial security would also reduce anger and frustration, as well as the need to continuously work second jobs to support short-term, emotionally generated purchases. Officers who have a sense of financial security are in a position to free themselves of anger and frustration at their employers and continue to invest energy into the professional goals that typified the earlier years of their careers. Providing ongoing training to police officers in the effective financial management of their personal lives reaps benefits in their professional lives.

Survivors Have Multiple Roles in Their Lives

One of the most difficult aspects of being a law enforcement officer is the need to strike a balance between being a highly effective law enforcement professional and at the same time an available friend, spouse, or parent outside the law enforcement role. This capacity to balance multiple significant emotional roles in one's life is the central defining aspect of an emotional survivor versus an emotional victim. The emotional victim, as previous chapters illuminate, is singularly defined by the police role. All emotional and psychological needs are closely linked to the law enforcement role. As demonstrated by case histories in previous chapters, the officer does not control the law enforcement role. If lack of control is one of the central components of the victim, then by definition the law enforcement officer whose life view is singularly defined by being a law enforcement officer is the most prone to being a victim. Many officers who have approached their entire law enforcement career enthusiastic, positively motivated, and highly energized about the job can unknowingly be victim-prone officers. Many times this victim-prone officer is operating from a perspective of emotional naiveté and unawareness of what could be lurking around the corner with any change in the organization. One example of a victim-prone officer is Commander Vasquez, in the following case study.

Case History

Commander Vasquez is an eighteen-year patrol-division commander of a medium-size police department. Throughout the course of his career, he has enthusiastically met every professional challenge that the organization has put before him. His average work week far exceeds the typical forty hours. Quite often several nights per week, he is available to the men and women of his command. He understands the basic tenets of leadership and practices them quite well. Commander Vasquez is easily the most respected member of the command staff at his organization. The men and women who work for him know that he cares about them, that he is an individual of honesty and integrity. The line personnel of the agency often say, "If you were disciplined by Commander Vasquez, you deserved it. He doesn't play games with the people who work for him." Commander Vasquez's career at one level is highly successful. He enjoys the respect of rank-and-file law enforcement officers as well as colleagues within the command

continued

staff. He pursued an advanced education over the course of his career, obtaining a master's degree in public administration. He is also fortunate enough to be able to attend the FBI National Academy in Quantico, Virginia, and has a significant network of law enforcement colleagues at a national level.

From all outside views, Commander Vasquez would be considered a successful law enforcement officer. During Commander Vasquez's eighteenth year of employment, however, the chief of police for whom he works retires and is replaced by an individual who was an assistant chief at a major city police department from another part of the country. Commander Vasquez has just begun his attendance at the FBI National Academy when the new chief arrives at his agency to assume the position of chief of police. Commander Vasquez's absence over the course of the new chief of police's first three months of tenure creates a situation in which the new chief of police has created friendships with several other members of the command staff and considers Commander Vasquez somewhat of an unknown entity and often refers to him at command meetings as "the commander we have back at the NA."

Upon returning from his three-month stint at the National Academy, Commander Vasquez finds he's been transferred to a new command position in another area of the agency. This particular transfer does not trouble Commander Vasquez, who views his position with the agency with flexibility, and he meets his new position with enthusiasm.

He realizes that he has been successful throughout his career by approaching his tasks with enthusiasm, motivation, and dedication to his position as a law enforcement commander. Although successful in his new command position, he begins noticing that the new chief of police operates from an ethical frame of reference that is somewhat different from what had typified the agency under the old chief of police. Commander Vasquez believes in operating above reproach and feels strongly that interaction with the public, subordinate officers, or command colleagues should always be predicated on honesty and integrity. It becomes quite apparent to him that the new chief of police values political loyalty and a network of sycophants more than professional integrity. Commander Vasquez, during executive retreats on more than one occasion, points out respectfully that programs the new chief is considering are somewhat self-serving for the police department and lack the sense of community need and integrity that Commander Vasquez believes are core to the manner in which the agency serves the public. The present chief advises him that it is not his concern whether the program is based on integrity or not and that Commander Vasquez should do what he is told if he wants to retain his command or the chief will find somebody else who would do it. Commander Vasquez at no point engages in disrespectful interaction with the chief, but he soon finds himself being removed from areas of professional responsibility that he values. A confidante advises Commander Vasquez that the new chief of police considers him untrustworthy.

While functioning as a force commander (a rotating temporary assignment that all command personnel do one shift per month), Commander Vasquez supervises the dispatching of patrol officers to the city manager's residence for a domestic violence incident. Upon arriving at the location of the call, Commander Vasquez is met by a patrol sergeant and three patrol officers who inform him that the city manager has physically assaulted his wife to the extent that she requires minor medical attention. Commander Vasquez reminds the patrol sergeant of the departmental policy and state statutes concerning domestic violence incidents and the need for a mandatory physical arrest of the city manager. The officers under Commander Vasquez's direction take the city manager into custody. He believes the arrest is absolutely appropriate, continued is based on probable cause and the evidence at the scene, and does not reflect either an absence of law enforcement action taken nor preferential treatment toward the city manager. Upon hearing of the physical arrest of the city manager, however, the chief of police informally admonishes Commander Vasquez, informing him that the organization has "an institutional memory."

During the next months, Commander Vasquez finds his evaluations reflect ratings of below satisfactory performance, a rating that he has never received in his prior eighteen years of law enforcement service. He believes that if he continues to use the traits of dedication, motivation, and integrity that have typified his career, he will soon convince the new chief of police that his performance as a law enforcement officer is based on integrity not politics. Quite obviously, he operates ethically and professionally from a different frame of reference than the new chief of police. Commander Vasquez continues to find himself embroiled in informal discipline and being professionally ostracized by the new chief. As the months continue and as he becomes convinced that the chief of police is an ethically bankrupt individual, Commander Vasquez's attitude toward the chief becomes confrontational. He begins assuming a rather defensive posture and eventually must retain an attorney to protect his professional position when the chief begins demotional proceedings against him for reasons lacking any objective foundation.

As the confrontation with the new chief develops and intensifies, it becomes quite apparent that Commander Vasquez lacks the emotional support systems that would typify an emotional survivor. His career has been highly successful, and he does not have any significant bumps in the road over the past two decades of being a law enforcement officer. He sees the department only in a positive light and believes he has always been treated fairly by the agency.

But for the first time in Commander Vasquez's life, he finds himself becoming disenchanted and angry, and he feels ostracized by the inner circle of individuals who now run the police department. He begins realizing that for the past eighteen years of his life, the police department has been his central focus. He has not developed significant support systems outside law enforcement. He does not have any friends outside law enforcement personnel. He does not belong to any established spiritual worship community. He does not have any driving recreational pursuits or a significant program of physical fitness.

As the confrontations with the chief of police and his band of sycophants begin increasing, Commander Vasquez finds himself ruminating and becoming obsessed with the way the new chief of police is treating him. He becomes quite agitated in his personal life. He begins experiencing a sleep disorder because he spends his nights contemplating what is taking place in his professional life, and he becomes increasingly enraged. In basic terms, Commander Vasquez has lived his entire life for the past two decades by putting all his emotional needs in the basket called police work, and now, for the first time in his career, he realizes he does not hold the handle to that basket—his career. All the skills that worked previously for Commander Vasquez—honesty, integrity, hard work, dedication, and motivation—do not enable him to overcome the burden of having to work for a basically politically dishonest chief of police. Retirement for Commander Vasquez is at a minimum three years in the future, and he does not appear to have any outlets other than police work in which to invest his energy. His life has turned from being basically a positive, enthusiastic one to a life consumed by anger, frustration, hostility, and resentment toward the way he is being treated by an agency that he was quite willing to say, a few years ago, that he loved.

Commander Vasquez's dilemma is not uncommon in law enforcement at all. Honest and dedicated law enforcement officers have a difficult time accepting political favoritism, cronyism, disloyalty, and dishonesty. Unfortunately, many good men and women can find themselves confronted with the paradox of being emotionally overinvested and defining themselves as law enforcement officers, yet at the same time beginning to hate the role. If you hate the role of police officer and at the same time you define yourself only by the role of police officer, you begin a cycle of self-hatred and destructiveness. Commander Vasquez clearly has significant deficits in non-police-related roles in his life. The emotional rollercoaster, as well as a basic love of police work, have combined to produce a deficiency of outside support systems in his life. Although Commander Vasquez is married, he and his wife have not established any ongoing social or recreational pursuits they share. She has her own profession, as does Commander Vasquez. They live rather independent lives. His two children are both away at college, and for the first time in his life, Commander Vasquez finds himself becoming angry, frustrated, and depressed about his present position. He looks forward to retirement, not so much from a position of enthusiasm for postretirement life, but mainly as a way to "get away from the chief."

Survivors have other roles in their lives. Although at the surface level, Commander Vasquez was successful, positive, and enthusiastic for most of his career, he is basically a victim waiting to happen. He does not have a significant amount of his life that is truly in his hands. Quite obviously he controls his dedication, his professionalism, and how well he does his job, but he does not have a well-developed social network outside of police work. He also does not have any recreational pursuits or physical fitness strategies to help him deal with the social and physical confrontations he is facing.

Quite often, law enforcement officers, when reviewing their career, will speak about a change from "loving the job" to "hating this place." Both attitudes likely typify overinvestment emotionally. Having a positive, enthusiastic dedication to police work while having a positive, enthusiastic dedication toward other aspects of one's life would typify balance, the central trait of the survivor. Keeping all emotional eggs in one basket, whether those are eggs marked "love" or marked "hate," is the central trait of the victim. Learning the skills to balance investment in the police role with investment in personal life roles is what defines a survivor. Having other roles in life that the officer truly controls reduces the feeling of vulnerability, helplessness, and being emotionally at risk to the agency that typifies many victim officers. The survivor has a balanced emotional investment portfolio. This investment continues over many years of productive police work. It's not so much that the survivor officer has learned to turn off police work at the end of the shift as it is that he or she has learned to turn on the other roles. The other roles are not merely pastimes or idle activities for the survivor law enforcement officers; they are truly emotionally invested dimensions in officers' lives. These other roles are dimensions of life in which the officers have a sense of passion and concern and, most important, control and self-determination.

> *If you hate the role of police officer and at the same time you define yourself only by the role of police officer, you begin a cycle of self-hatred and destructiveness.*

Decide to Survive

Being the best law enforcement officer one can be is important to the survivor officer, but so is being

- the best mother or father
- the best husband or wife
- the best community member
- the best golfer
- the best fly fisherman
- the best little league coach
- the best scout leader

The officers who make police work their lives are only coasting through a career and really don't have a strategy to be emotional survivors. They are only hoping that they don't get screwed by

- the agency
- the chief
- the sheriff
- the special agent in charge

They forget the one basic rule about the police career:

Nobody, but nobody, escapes with their professional virginity intact. Everyone gets screwed at least one time.

Survivors place the central issues in their lives in their own control. They understand what they control and what the agency controls. Once officers reach the point of being emotional survivors, they experience a significant reduction in anxiety and defensiveness. They focus on being the best officers they can be and then move on to more important things. Survivors make decisions from their core values, not from situational values, so they are typically free of facing significant disciplinary attention. On occasion, even though they are deserving of it, they are not promoted, or they are not chosen for the assignment they would like to have received, but they are still the most successful officers. Emotional survivors may appear to finish in last place, but that is because they are usually running a different race.

Becoming an emotional survivor can be a decision an officer makes at any point in a law enforcement career. On occasion, even a retired law enforcement professional must learn the strategies and attributes of becoming an emotional survivor to undo emotional damage that developed years, even decades, before. Police families can

> *Survivors place the central issues in their lives in their own control. They understand what they control and what the agency controls.*

practice the skills of being survivor families, putting the priorities and events of the lives of family members well above the events taking place at the law enforcement agency. The journey through a law enforcement career does not have to lead to the devastation and loss that it so often does. Just as law enforcement professionals practice street survival, they must practice emotional survival—they only need to be shown and mentored and modeled across the years of service.

The Officer's Legacy

In looking at how many officers live life as either victims or survivors, I'd like to point out two cases of two good officers making very different choices.

Case History

A chief of a medium-size police agency calls to ask me to help the family of a terminally ill officer. The chief relates that his officer has but a few weeks remaining to live and is requesting that his twenty-five-year-old son come to the hospice so the officer can make his peace with his son and say goodbye. The chief relates to me that the son has not spoken to his father since the son turned eighteen and left home after some turbulent teenage years. The chief had spoken to the son and attempted on his own to convince him to visit his father, but on each occasion the son refused. The chief asks if I would attempt to convince the son to see his dying father.

I travel for a day to meet with the son. I arrive unannounced at the son's home and ask to speak with him. Upon introducing myself and telling the son that I am there to talk to him about his father, the son states, "You're here to tell me my father's dead, aren't you?"

I reply, "No, but you really ought to go see him."

To this rather inappropriate statement, the son becomes enraged and begins yelling at me to leave, saying I have

continued

no right to impose my opinion on matters that do not pertain to me. The son becomes physically threatening and tells me, "Get off my place before I kick your ass!"

After I tell him I've traveled a few hundred miles to talk to him about this, the son backs off and says, "Well, hell, you came that far. I'll listen to what you have to say." The son, however, does the talking:

"You want to know about my father, well, I'll tell you about my father. The only thing I remember about him growing up was I was constantly told if I didn't straighten up, I was going to grow up to be a 'total asshole.' I have no memory of him helping me with school, coming to any of my football or basketball games, or anything. Hell, he was always too busy with his damn police work. When I got old enough to not have to take his bullshit anymore, things got real tense around the house. I left home the day after graduation from high school, and I haven't spoken a word to him since then, and I have no intention of talking to him now. I'm sorry he's real sick, but it just isn't my problem. I closed the book on him seven years ago, and I'm not going to open it again."

I talk to him for close to three hours, and the young man doesn't budge an inch. I tell him, "It would take you about fifteen minutes out of your way to stop at the hospice and see your father. If it is a total waste of time, as you think it will be for you, then all you've wasted is fifteen minutes; but when your father is gone, you'll never get that chance again." To this, the son replies, "I'm not going to give it fifteen seconds. The book is closed. You tell my mother that when he is gone, I'll help her any way I can."

Despite my attempts and discussion, the son refuses to see his father, and I leave unsuccessful. After seeing the son, I talk with the chief who had requested my involvement and ask him to tell me about his officer.

The chief replies, "I don't know what the hell is wrong with that son of his. My officer is one of the best men I have ever known in my lifetime. He is a caring and compassionate person. He is active in our school programs working with kids. He is involved in our officers' association and helps put on a toy drive every Christmas for the poor kids in our town, and every Thanksgiving, he and a handful of other officers help sponsor a food drive and pass out boxes of food and turkeys to families that can't afford a holiday meal. I just don't know what the hell is wrong with that boy of his."

I say I am sorry I couldn't convince the son to visit his father and leave to begin the trip back home. While traveling home, I reflect on why the son wouldn't visit the hospice to see his father. Despite the conflicts that had previously existed, the son's visit would make the officer's last days more comfortable by possibly enabling the officer to have closure and maybe discuss and try to make amends for the difficulties that typified their father-son relationship. I later learn from the chief that the father-son meeting never took place. It seems like such a waste. How do two people become so estranged? I wonder if the officer, whom the chief of police described as a compassionate man who cared about people, was the same man the son knew. Was the chief describing the man at the top of the rollercoaster and the son describing the man at the bottom? Did they even know the same person?

Not long after the case history above takes place, a police agency requests that I assist in the death notification of an officer who died in a motor vehicle accident while in another city. I go to the home along with the chief of police and a chaplain. The young woman being told her husband will never come home again is approximately thirty-five years old with two adolescent children.

I visit with the family several times during the next few months. Obviously, she is devastated and overwhelmed by the emotional trauma of the situation, but her support systems of family, friends, and fellow church members appear to be immensely helping her deal with her grief and loss.

On one visit to the home, I need to borrow the family telephone to return a call. In the kitchen, I notice a small placard taped under the wall-mounted telephone that reads:

"This is a Career not a Crusade"

I ask the widow about the placard's meaning, and she responds: "Oh, I should take that down, but I just don't have the courage. My husband put it up there, half as a joke and half as a reminder. It started down at the agency, where he had pictures of his family on his desk, and some of the other detectives had pictures of loads of narcotics they had seized—you know the cops call them 'glory shots.' He had the family pictures on his desk, and they teased him about it. The other guys at the agency put up a little sign that said, 'So much Cocaine, such little Time,' and that was when my husband put up the sign at the office: 'This is a Career not a Crusade.' It all started as a joke, but I think it was pretty serious to him.

"He loved working as a cop, but he saw so many of his friends lose marriages and families. They all would go out for a beer after work. My husband would go most of the time, but he was usually the first to leave and come home.

He really loved being a cop, but you know, he always remembered the family. I might forget a birthday, anniversary, or something. He never did. If he had to work on Thanksgiving, then we had our meal the day before or the day after, but we had our Thanksgiving as a family. Our Christmas might be December 23 because of his job, but we had our family Christmas. I think he made just about every parent-teacher meeting or school event; some he couldn't make, but he sure tried. I miss him terribly, but I had such a wonderful life with him."

As I listen to this young widow recounting her husband's life as an officer and as a father and husband, I am struck by just one word of her story:

"I had such a wonderful life with him."

On other occasions, I have spoken to spouses or parents who have lost law enforcement loved ones, and the words are often different than those spoken by the widow in the above case history. So often the words are "I miss him terribly, and he could have retired last year, and then we were going to have our time," or "In five years we were going to retire and move upstate, and then it would be our time." This young woman in the above case history told a story of an excellent law enforcement officer who must have seen life as a survivor. They *had* such a wonderful life together. They lived in the present. They took advantage of every moment of their family and personal time, and at the same time he was a highly productive officer. He apparently had the strategies to break the rollercoaster. His life was full, and he left a family that missed and valued him.

The question could be asked:

"Which officer loved his family and children more, the officer in the first case whose son wouldn't visit him as he died, or the second officer, who saw police work as a 'career not a crusade'?"

In my opinion, they *both* loved their families and children. They were probably both good, decent men and hard-working law enforcement officers. Unfortunately, one didn't have an orientation through training in emotional survival and his victim outlook came into the home and destroyed his relationship with his son. The other officer left a wife and two children who knew he loved them, not just with his emotions, but also with his behavior and time. The second officer's child is presently a law enforcement officer at the father's agency. The second officer knew how to break the roller-coaster and live life. Although tragically he died too young, he lived life as a survivor.

About the Author

Dr. Kevin M. Gilmartin, author of the book *Emotional Survival for Law Enforcement: A Guide for Officers and Their Families*, is a behavioral scientist specializing in law enforcement and public safety-related issues. He previously spent twenty years working in law enforcement in Tucson, Arizona. During his tenure, he supervised the Hostage Negotiations Team and the Behavioral Sciences Unit. He is a recipient of the IACP National Police Officer Service Award for contributions during hostage negotiations.

He presently maintains a consulting relationship with public safety and law enforcement agencies in the U.S., Canada, and Australia. He has held adjunct faculty positions with the University of Massachusetts (Lowell) Police Leadership Institute, Cornell University New York State School of Industrial and Labor Relations, Sam Houston State University Law Enforcement Management Institute of Texas, and the University of Arizona. He has been a guest instructor at the FBI Academy in Quantico, Virginia for over thirty years.

The Department of Justice, FBI, Royal Canadian Mounted Police, Police Service of New South Wales, and the International Association of Chiefs of Police have published his work. He holds a doctoral degree in clinical psychology from the University of Arizona and is a licensed psychologist in Arizona. He is a veteran of the U.S. Marine Corps and resides in Tucson, Arizona, and Sunriver, Oregon. He can be reached by email at ghakev@aol.com, or through the book's website, www.EmotionalSurvival.com.